Access to History
General Editor: Keith Randell

The Tsars, Russia, Poland and the Ukraine 1462–1725

Martyn Rady

Hodder & Stoughton

A MEMBER OF THE HODDER HEADLINE GROUP

The cover illustration shows a portrait of Peter the Great (By gracious permission of HM the Queen)

British Library Cataloguing in Publication Data
Rady, Martyn C.
  The Tsars, Russia, Poland and the Ukraine 1462–1725 —
  (Access to History).
  1. Eastern Europe, 1740–1980
  I. Title II. Series
  947

ISBN 0 340 53258 0

First published 1990
Impression number   10 9 8 7 6 5 4 3
Year   1999 1998 1997

Typeset by Wearset, Boldon, Tyne and Wear.
Printed in Great Britain for Hodder & Stoughton Educational, a division of Hodder Headline Plc, 338 Euston Road, London NW1 3BH by Athenaeum Press Ltd, Gateshead, Tyne and Wear.

Contents

Preface

This series is intended to provide a concise and easily accessible guide to a range of historical topics and periods, both for the general reader and the student.

For the history student, study guides at the end of each chapter provide diagrammatic summaries of the key points, advice on note taking and advice on handling essay questions. In addition, examples of appropriate source-based questions are given, relating to the primary source material that is woven into the text. To assist with understanding, a * is inserted at various points in the text where a break for a re-read and note making is recommended.

For both general readers and students who wish to pursue their understanding and study of the topic further, a brief selection of suggestions for further reading is included at the end of the book.

A Note on 'Muscovy' and 'Russia'

'Muscovy' and 'Russia' are not synonymous, although they are often treated as such. Until the eighteenth century, 'Russia' might be used to mean either the territory in which the Russian people lived or those lands which had formerly been a part of the medieval Kievan–Russian state. Since ethnic boundaries were fluid and the Kievan state was soon only a distant memory, the territories pertaining to 'Russia' were not firmly fixed. 'Muscovy' is, by contrast, a political term and refers to the region ruled over by the princes of Muscovy from the capital city of Moscow. In 1721, Peter the Great commanded that Muscovy be henceforward known as the 'Russian Empire'. Since by the early eighteenth century, the area belonging to Muscovy extended over nearly all the region previously known as Russia, it makes sense to follow Peter's instruction.

CHAPTER 1

Background

1 Land and Climate

The history of eastern Europe rests on its geography. Both Poland and European Russia lie on the broadest part of the European Plain. It is almost a thousand miles from the Black Sea to the Gulf of Finland, and twice this distance separates the Ural mountains from Poland's modern boundary with Germany on the River Oder. Yet in the whole of this vast space, the ground seldom rises much above a thousand feet. Although the countryside is far from uniform, containing a diversity of forests, waterways, cultivated land and pasture, the overall impression is one of flatness relieved only by low, rolling, inclines. 'The whole country is plain and champaign [level land] and has few hills in it', was the comment of an English traveller who passed this way in the sixteenth century. 'Flat, empty, regular, without colour, without bounds but even so without grandeur', is how a nineteenth-century French visitor dismissed the dull Russian landscape.

The rivers which traverse European Russia and Poland flow for the most part in a north–south direction, intersecting the lowlands before debouching variously into the Baltic and the Black Seas. Nevertheless, by reason of its flatness, this part of the European plain offers relatively easy passage for armies. Even in the more forested parts, an army may make good progress along the straight roads which cut through the woods and clearings. The tide of invasion has always flowed strongly in this part of Europe and since antiquity the 'peoples of the plains' have in turns been victors and vanquished. Land, which is the chief spoil of war, has in the course of these struggles passed from Germans, to Poles and to Russians, with much toing and froing in between. With each change in the order of ascendancy, the political map of eastern Europe has been drastically redrawn.

Despite the apparent consistency of its contours, there is nothing uniform about the climate or vegetation in this part of Europe. Both Poland and Russia have a 'continental climate', suffering from extremes of temperature in summer and winter. Poland, however, lies sufficiently westwards to benefit from the moderating influence of the Gulf Stream, the belt of warm, moist air which flows off the Atlantic. Accordingly, Poland's winters are less harsh than those of Russia, and her summers are less arid. In Warsaw, the capital of Poland, which lies on the same latitude as Birmingham, the average daytime temperature in January is −3°C. Moscow, located on the same latitude as Edinburgh, has an average noonday temperature in winter of −12°C. For six

The European Plain.
Map shows political boundaries after 1945

months of the year the ground is frozen solid. By contrast, the Ukraine, the cornbelt which has its counterpart in the North American prairie, suffers because of its easterly location from regular periods of drought.

  ★ Ibrahim-ibn-Jakub, a tenth-century Arab geographer, described

See Preface for explanation of ★ symbol.

Poland as containing 'the richest limits of land suitable for settlement and most plentiful in means of support'. Ibn-Jakub's report most probably refers to Great Poland, which lies between the river courses of the upper Oder and middle Vistula. To this day, Great Poland is a fertile open country of meadowlands and brooks, yielding, as in the tenth century, 'an abundance of food, meat, honey and fish'. To the south of Great Poland lies Little Poland, which backs on to the Carpathian mountains. The hillier terrain of Little Poland provides opportunities for cattle-rearing and vine-growing, and its agricultural economy thus complements Great Poland's. However, as one proceeds eastwards from Poland, the vegetation becomes progressively less luxuriant. Eventually, the meadows and pastures are replaced by the spruce forests of Prussia on the Baltic and by the waterlogged soil of White Russia (Belorussia). Although long fought over by Poles, Germans, Russians and others, Prussia and White Russia are poorer in natural resources than the lands which lie to the west. Oats, rye and flax make up their staple crops, and much of this region is, even to this day, unsuitable for farming.

   * The Ukraine, which lies to the south-east of Poland and White Russia, is a fabled land of plenty. It sits on a belt of fertile soil, so rich in humus that it is almost black. Although given to drought in summer, the Ukraine is good farming country, having in the seventeenth century, 'fields as blissful as the Elysian and so many cattle, wild animals and various birds that one could think this the birthplace of Diana'. Great slugs of rivers, the Dniester, Dnieper and Don, flow southwards through the Ukraine on their way to the Black Sea. Along these waterways came the first 'Russians' who in the ninth century founded the city of Kiev.

   The Ukraine lies on the western part of the Russian steppes, the undulating grassland which reaches deep into central Asia. 'A wide, boundless plain . . . one drives on and on and cannot discern where it begins or where it ends', is how the novelist Chekhov described the expanse of the Russian steppes in the nineteenth century. Throughout the ancient and medieval periods, the steppes acted as a corridor along which wandering and predatory tribes passed, drawn westwards from Asia by the double-prospect of plunder and of more fertile pastures. Later, in the sixteenth and seventeenth centuries, bands of Cossacks marauded freely here. The vulnerability of the Ukraine to invasion for a long time made the region unattractive to settlers. The early Russians referred to the open spaces of the Ukraine as 'the field of fear'. For safety's sake, they preferred to dwell in the more sheltered forest region to the north. Despite its natural wealth, therefore, the Ukraine remained only thinly settled until the eighteenth century.

   * North of the Ukraine, European Russia is crossed by thick tracts of forest. Around Novgorod and St Petersburg (Leningrad) pines predominate. In the Moscow region, deciduous varieties—oak, birch and

hornbeam—compete with conifers. The denseness of the Russian forests and the bleakness of the wooded landscape has never ceased to excite resentful comment from foreign travellers. A Venetian envoy, who journeyed through the region in the fifteenth century, recorded how, 'from the 21st of January when we left Moscow, until the 12th of February when we reached Troki [in Lithuania], we travelled continually through forests. Sometimes we found a village where we rested, but usually slept in the forest'. Some 350 years later, the Marquis de Custine, whose carriage broke down every 20 miles on the rutted roads, dismissed this part of Russia as 'strewn as far as the eye can see with poor, miserable birch trees'. For the modern day traveller, able to survey the countryside from the relative comfort of the Moscow–Leningrad express, the abiding impression remains one of stark woodland, broken only by the occasional clearing and settlement.

Notwithstanding these incidental impressions, much of the forest zone has over the course of time been pressed into agricultural service. However, the fertile black soil extends only a little way into the forests. All the rest is a clay soil so lacking in humus for the Russians to call it grey. The deficiencies of the soil are compounded by the length and harshness of the winters. In the forest region of Russia, the growing season is foreshortened, averaging only five months a year as against western Europe's eight or nine. Agricultural production is correspondingly low. In the late middle ages the Russian grain-yield per acre is estimated to have been only half of that achieved farther west.

Despite the disadvantages of the forested part of Russia, it was here, 'in the cold solitudes of the Christian East . . . in this sad land, vast like the Ocean' (De Custine), that the principality of Muscovy was formed. Over the course of the late middle ages, Muscovy embarked on a course of territorial expansion, swallowing up its neighbours and bringing most of the forested region under its sway. Then, in the sixteenth century, Muscovy burst forth from the treeline, pressing outwards towards Poland and the open spaces of the Ukraine. From this mighty movement came the Russian Empire, progenitor of the modern-day Soviet superpower.

2 The Dark Ages

The Dark Ages, the period of European history extending from the fall of the Roman Empire to the end of the first millenium, are not so called because life was particularly grim or grisly then. 'Dark' refers simply to the gloom in which the historian must work in trying to establish what was actually happening during this time. In the pages of monastic chronicles, the historian of the Dark Ages will encounter the names of battles and of kings, but the causes of conflict and the motives of the rulers will seldom be revealed. The farther eastwards one looks, the less the information available. For most of the first millenium, eastern

Europe was entirely pagan and so beyond the reach of the Christian clergy: the only literate group capable of leaving an account of their experiences. All the historian has therefore for written sources are odd fragments of tales, and his work of reconstruction must necessarily proceed as much by guesswork as by patient documentary research.

The dominant racial and linguistic group in eastern Europe is Slav. Slavs make up most of the present population of Poland, Czechoslovakia, Yugoslavia, Bulgaria and European Russia, including the Ukraine. The Slavs' original home is uncertain, although most probably it lay in the area north of the Carpathian mountains. During the seventh and eighth centuries of our era, the Slav population began to disperse across a wide geographical region. As a consequence of this movement three separate Slavonic groups were formed: the Southern Slavs who occupied the Balkans; the Eastern Slavs who moved into Russia; and the Western Slavs who migrated into the area of modern-day Poland and Czechoslovakia (see map on page 6). In their new regions of settlement, the Slavs intermingled with the native Celtic, Thracian and Finnic populations. As a result of this process of dispersal and intermixing, the languages spoken by the Slav people began to differ from one another and even to subdivide within themselves. Owing to the absence of any written survivals of the Slavonic language from this period, the process of linguistic fragmentation cannot be traced with any precision.

★ The Slavs subsisted in the main from fighting and farming and their earliest settlements took the form of isolated clusters of villages, often built around earthworks. Gradually though, over the course of the ninth century, a rudimentary political organization began to weld together the individual Slav communities. The origins of what later became the Bohemian and Serbian kingdoms have been traced back by historians to this early period of state-foundation. At about the same time, a Slav chieftain called Piast founded a principality known as Polania in the region north of the Carpathians. Under Piast's successors, the territories making up Polania extended from Pomerania on the Baltic to the upper reaches of the Vistula river. Perhaps remote ninth-century Polania is the 'Vistula-land' mysteriously referred to in King Alfred of England's *Geography*: 'To the east of Moravia is Vistula-land [Visle land] and eastwards of Vistula-land is Dacia where the Goths live.'

The history of Polania becomes a good deal less obscure as we move into the tenth century. Plainly, by this time the rulers of the Piast dynasty were finding it hard to maintain their grip on Polania. In the western regions of Polanian territory, Piast control was challenged by the expansionist drive of German princelings, the nominal subjects of the Holy Roman Emperor. To counter this threat, the Piast ruler was eventually forced into taking a momentous step. In AD 966 Prince Mieszko of Polania resolved to embrace Christianity. He hoped by this measure to cement a political partnership sufficient to put a halt to

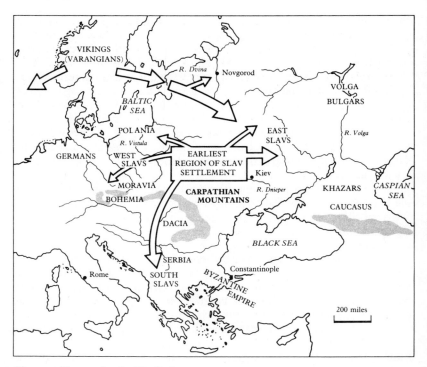

Eastern Europe in the Dark Ages

further German expansion eastward. In the event, while Mieszko may have preserved his country's independence, his conversion brought Polania into the cultural and religious orbit of Catholic Christendom. Bishops and monks established themselves in the Polanian lands, undertaking the conversion of the populace, and crowns were sent by both Emperor and Pope so that the ruler of Polania might henceforward consider himself a king. Out of the pagan principality of Polania, was thus born the Catholic kingdom of Poland.

  * Developments among the Eastern Slavs followed a rather different course. The Slavs who settled along the Dnieper and Dvina rivers were swiftly drawn into close trading relations with the Turkic tribes of Khazars and Bulgars, which constituted the most advanced political and economic force in the region. Dealing in furs, honey, wax and slaves, the Slav tribes of what is now European Russia and the Ukraine soon established a network of commercial centres wherein they exchanged their local wares for silk and metals. Possibly as many as 600 small towns sprang up to meet the commercial requirements of the

region, hence the earliest name given to the land of the Eastern Slavs: *Gaardariki*, 'the kingdom of the towns'.

The wealth of *Gaardariki* soon attracted the attention of the Slavs' northern neighbours. From their communities along the Baltic shore, Viking or Varangian chieftains began to penetrate the hinterland. In AD 862 the Varangian Roderick (or Rurik) seized the Slav town of Novgorod. By the close of the century, Roderick's successors had extended their sway as far south as Kiev. The city of Kiev, which lies on the edge of the black-earth country, and stands at the place where the forests of the north give way to the open spaces of the Ukraine, became the Varangians' most important stronghold in the East Slav lands. The trade routes passing from the Baltic to the Black Sea and the Caspian, all of which passed near Kiev, soon fell under Varangian control. The Varangians called their newly-acquired territories *Rus*. From this Scandinavian word, which means 'land of the seafarers', derives the name of Russia.

3 Kievan Russia and its Neighbours

The Varangian interest in the East Slav lands was at first almost entirely commercial. In its origin, *Kiev-Rus* or 'Kievan Russia', as it is commonly known by historians, was little more than a business enterprise set up for the purposes of extracting trade and tribute. Nevertheless, over the course of the tenth century, the Varangian enterprise in the Russian lands rapidly acquired the characteristics of a venture in state-building. Within a few decades of their arrival, the Varangian conquerors had established peaceful relations with the tribes dwelling in the region. Soon they intermarried with the native women-folk and adopted Russian as their language even to the extent of giving up their old Scandinavian names. Roderick thus became Rurik, Ingwarr became Igor, and Waldemar became Vladimir. The conversion of Russia to Christianity in AD 988 greatly hastened the political development of the region. Firstly, Christianity bound both ruler and subjects in a common religious loyalty which largely obliterated past distinctions. Secondly, the Christian priesthood of Russia, headed by a 'Metropolitan' of Kiev, supported the work of government by helping in the preparation of legal codes, by undertaking the 'civilizing' task of evangelism in the countryside, and by educating a core of future administrators.

In contrast to Poland–Polania, which had been converted to Catholicism, the Christianity adopted in Russia was of the orthodox variety. Monks from Byzantium and the Balkans founded the first monasteries and bishoprics, and undertook the training of a native clergy. In its law and ritual, its icons and architecture, the Russian church looked not to Catholic Rome but to Greek Constantinople. As a consequence of this, the Metropolitan of Kiev, the highest dignitary in the Russian ecclesias-

Kievan Russia

tical hierarchy, was until the sixteenth century appointed by the Greek Patriarch of Constantinople.

★ By way of its orthodox church and clergy, Kievan Russia gradually became acquainted with the idea of government and kingship practised in the Byzantine or East Roman Empire. The Emperor of Byzantium was regarded by his subjects as possessing a divine authority: 'Though an Emperor be in body like all others, yet in the power of his office he is like God, Master of all men'. In the whole of the Byzantine Empire, no institution served to check the Emperor's will; his word was the law and he was held answerable only to God. Even the church was regarded as a subordinate branch of imperial government.

Following the conversion of Russia to Christianity, similar ideas of 'theocratic kingship' began to take root in the Kievan state. In the rituals of their coronation, and in their robes and insignia of office, the princes of Kiev self-consciously imitated the Byzantine rulers. Chronicles and religious texts further illustrated the close links between the prince and the Emperor, and Byzantine forms of address began to be applied to the ruler. Whether this exalted theory of monarchy was ever translated into the actual practice of government, and whether the prince of Kievan Russia exercised a form of autocratic rule over his subjects, are issues on which the surviving documents shed little light.

* Throughout the early history both of Kievan Russia and of Poland, no distinction was made between the public and private property of the ruling dynasty. Instead, the state was regarded as a family possession, belonging to the reigning house, which on the prince's death would be shared out among his relatives. With the passage of generations, therefore, the unity of the Polish and Russian lands was steadily weakened as ever smaller units of territory were created on the death of each ruler. Although it was usual both in Poland and in Russia for one prince to retain a nominal sovereignty over all the rest, the process of partition led inexorably to political enfeeblement and to squabbling for land. As a consequence, Poland and Russia rapidly fell victim to internal strife and to foreign invasion.

In Poland the process of territorial fragmentation began within 40 years of the death of Mieszko, the country's first Christian king. Only in the mid-twelfth century did the pace of division slacken. By this time, Poland had broken up into five virtually independent duchies. While in theory, Poland still had a sovereign who ruled from the capital city of Cracow, his power extended only over Little Poland. Elsewhere, the reigning dukes barely admitted his authority. The confused circumstances of this period may explain why Polish documents issued in the twelfth and thirteenth centuries seldom agree as to whether Poland had at its head a prince, a king or a duke. Even in the fourteenth century, an English traveller might still refer to Poland variously as 'the land of Polayne' and 'the realm of Cracow'.

* In Kievan Russia, a similar but far bloodier process of fragmentation took place. Over the course of the eleventh and twelfth centuries, Russia disintegrated into about a dozen separate principalities over which rival members of the House of Rurik (the descendants of the Varangian Roderick) fought for control. One Russian historian has estimated that, of the 150 years from 1074 to 1223, some 80 witnessed civil war.

The prolonged period of partition and civil strife dealt a severe blow to the city of Kiev. During the twelfth century, Kiev gradually lost its political importance as new centres of influence were established within the Russian lands. To the west, the principality of Volhynia–Galicia, lying in the folds of the Carpathians, embarked upon its brief period of splendour. In the far north, the inland port of Novgorod acquired the basis of its political independence and mercantile wealth which was to ensure its survival as a self-governing and prosperous city-state in the centuries to come.

Although Russia still had a few vigorous centres of political and economic influence, endemic civil discord made it an easy prey to conquest from the east. During the late eleventh and twelfth centuries, bands of Cuman nomads from Asia broke into Russia, having made their way westwards along the 'steppe corridor'. The disunited Russian princes were increasingly unable to resist the assaults of the pagan horsemen from the east and they did not heed the words of the Cuman envoys and captives who attended their courts. For the Cumans were themselves in desperate flight from a new and powerful adversary pressing hard against them in the east. This was the Empire of the Mongol–Tatars.

4 The Mongol–Tatar Inheritance

During the first decades of the thirteenth century, the Mongol chieftain Ghenghis Khan welded together a powerful tribal empire which extended across Mongolia, Manchuria and Eastern Siberia. The Mongol–Tatar Empire, as this confederation of Mongol and Turkic tribes is known to history, had within a short time conquered China and the Muslim states of Central Asia, even as far westwards as the Caspian Sea and the Caucasus mountains.

In 1223, the Mongol–Tatars broke for the first time into Kievan Russia, defeating a mixed band of Russians and Cumans on the River Kalka. Just as suddenly, the tribesmen withdrew, and for a time the Russians imagined themselves safe from further attack. However, in 1236 the grandson of Ghenghis Khan, Batu Khan, who had inherited the western part of the Mongol–Tatar Empire, crossed the Urals. In that year, Batu smashed the Volga Bulgars and advanced his army into the heart of Kievan Russia. The city of Kiev fell in 1240; Galicia, Poland and Hungary were overrun the next year. The advance guard of the invading host even reached the shores of the Adriatic.

The destruction wreaked by the Mongol–Tatars is amply described in the *Tale of the Ravage of Riazan by Batu*, composed shortly after the terrible onslaught: 'The churches of God they devastated, and in the holy altars they shed much blood. And no one in the town [of Riazan] remained alive: all died equally and drank the single cup of death. There was no one here to moan or cry . . . but all lay together dead'. Nor was the anonymous author exaggerating the scale of the devastation. When a papal envoy visited Kiev a few years after its capture, he found only 200 buildings left upright. Everywhere he noted mounds of human skulls and bones and burnt-out ruins.

Batu's capital lay at Sarai on the River Volga (see map on page 8). For reasons of security, and to keep a watchful eye on his relatives,

Batu was not ready to transfer his headquarters permanently to Europe. Since most of the territories he had conquered lay at too great a distance to be effectively administered from Sarai, Batu relinquished his grip over them. No such impediment spared the nearby lands of Kievan Russia. Kiev and the open spaces of the Ukraine were incorporated within the Mongol–Tatar 'Golden Horde' (as the empire of Batu's successors was known) and placed under the immediate control of governors appointed by the Khan. Elsewhere in Russia, the surviving rulers were retained and obliged to act as collectors of taxes and tribute. In order to preserve what was left of their authority, the Russian princes were additionally compelled to promise full allegiance to their new overlord and to receive from him their seals of office.

The long period of the 'Tatar yoke', the 300 years (c. 1240–1540) during which Russia lay under Mongol–Tatar suzerainty, exercised a decisive effect upon the history of the region. Previously, Russia had enjoyed close commercial contacts with the west, acting as the intermediary through which goods from Byzantium and the Orient were passed to the rest of Europe. Certainly, Novgorod and, to a lesser extent, Pskov and Smolensk, continued to maintain trading relations with the regions lying to the west. However, commercial links between Europe and the other parts of Russia were severed. Even in England, the sudden loss of contact was felt, albeit indirectly. For no longer did German merchants purchase cargoes of herring in Great Yarmouth for resale in Russia. As for the native rulers of Russia, who had previously maintained close political and diplomatic contacts with the west, they were now reduced to the condition of vassals serving an Asian overlord. Thus, within the space of a few years, Kievan Russia was dramatically overthrown, and its lands and peoples transformed into outlying provinces and subjects of the Mongol–Tatar Golden Horde.

* Ever since the middle ages, the rulers of Russia have been autocrats, exercising their power despotically and without reference to representative institutions. The establishment of communist rule having made no appreciable difference to this trend, many historians have asked whether there may not be a tendency towards autocracy so deeply rooted in Russia's historical experience as to prevent the establishment of any other system of government.

Although the origins of Russian autocracy are still debated, a number of historians would agree that they may be traced back to the experience of Tatar rule. The Russian princes were regular visitors to the Tatar capital of Sarai, and they acted as functionaries of the Khan in the matter of collecting taxes. They thus became acquainted at first hand with the methods and ideology of oriental despotism, with its administrative techniques, and with the sort of authority 'with which one cannot enter into agreements but must unconditionally obey'. The Russian vocabulary continued even to this day to bear witness to Mongol–Tatar influences. The words for treasury and money (*kazna* and *denga*) derive directly from Mongol–Tatar names and reveal the Russian debt to the Tatars for their early financial institutions (themselves borrowed from the Chinese). More strikingly, the Russian language of repression has unmistakably oriental roots. The Russian for chains, whip, slavery and execution are all of Mongol–Tatar provenance. The Tatar conception of sovereignty, with its idea that the ruler possessed an unlimited authority, also seems to have been copied by their Russian vassals. As one visitor to the court of a Russian prince later reported, 'He [the prince] holds boundless control over the lives and property of his subjects: not one of his counsellors has sufficient authority to oppose him, or even to differ from him on any subject . . .'. Almost identical descriptions survive of the authority and power vested in the Tatar Khan. 'Whenever, whatever, whoever the Khan orders, be it war, life or death, is obeyed without contradiction': such was the comment of a papal envoy who visited the Khan's court in the fourteenth century.

Even though the Mongol–Tatars were converted from tribal worship to Islam in the early fourteenth century, they never showed much interest in spreading their own beliefs among the native Russians. Thus, the orthodox faith continued to be practised in Russia. Indeed, in return for the orthodox clergy remembering the Khan in their prayers, the Mongol–Tatars were prepared to exempt the church from tax payments. It was largely as a result of this concession that the orthodox church became the greatest landowner and repository of wealth in the whole of the Russian lands.

Unlike the situation in western Europe, where Pope and clergy exercised influence and authority quite independently of the secular rulers, the church in Russia advanced and strengthened the power of the prince. The orthodox priesthood continued throughout the period of Tatar overlordship to support the notion of theocratic kingship. This idea, which originated in Greek Byzantium, held that the ruler was appointed directly by God and that he functioned as a mouthpiece of the Almighty. 'They [the Russians] openly confess that the will of the prince is the will of God; on account of this they call him God's key-bearer and chamberlain, and in short they believe he is the executor of the divine will', was the comment of one western visitor to late medieval Russia. Owing to the Mongol–Tatars' tolerant attitude in the matter of their vassals' religion, orthodox notions of sovereignty thus survived and eventually fused with ideas on government deriving immediately from Tatar practices. In this way, theocratic kingship and oriental despotism jointly provided the foundation of Russian autocracy and of a view concerning the nature of civil authority which has persisted into the modern period.

5 Poland, Lithuania and the Teutonic Knights

All that the Mongol–Tatars demanded of the Russian princes was their prompt payment of tribute and their promises of loyalty. Providing these were given, the Khan was little concerned with who ruled where and over what. Accordingly, the imposition of the 'Tatar yoke' did little to stop the Russian princes from fighting among themselves. On top of this, the slow decline of the Mongol–Tatar Empire, starting in the mid-fourteenth century, added a new measure of insecurity to the politics of the region. Neighbouring powers moved into the vacuum created by the prolonged period of Mongol–Tatar weakness. Foremost among these were the Poles and the Lithuanians, and ranged behind these two lay a third force: the Teutonic Knights.

During the reigns of Wladyslaw the Short (1306–33) and Casimir the Great (1333–70) much of Poland was reunited under a single ruler, and the monarchy was restored to strength. Therewith, Poland began to expand south-eastwards, into the territories once belonging to Kievan Russia and still under nominal Tatar suzerainty. In the 1340s King Casimir annexed Galicia, and in 1366 he took Lodomeria and parts of Podolia. By reason of these accomplishments, Casimir adopted the proud title 'Lord of Russia' (*dominus et haeres Russiae*). As it turned out, however, Poland was at this time not the only power with an expansionist interest in the region.

* The Lithuanians were a Baltic people, racially distinct from the Slavs, although speaking a tongue which shares a remote common ancestry with the Slavonic language. Their original home was along the eastern shores of the Baltic Sea. However, during the thirteenth and fourteenth centuries the Lithuanians established a state of considerable power and size which extended over a large part of eastern Europe. Unlike the neighbouring Poles and Russians, the Lithuanians were pagans, being worshippers of Perkun, the God of the Thunderclap. Because they resisted all attempts at conversion, the Lithuanians soon attracted the attention of the crusading Teutonic Knights.

* The Order of Teutonic Knights had been founded at the time of the crusades to help the fight against the infidel in the Holy Land. Although the Order's warriors might on the battlefield behave no differently from other soldiers, beneath their armour the Knights were monks. All had upon entering the Order sworn oaths of chastity, poverty and obedience. Like other monks, the Knights wore a habit: a white tunic adorned with a black cross. They lived communally, eating in refectories and sleeping in dormitories. But whereas other monks would devote most of their waking hours to prayer and meditation, the monks of the Teutonic Order engaged in the hard, physical struggle against the unbeliever.

The Saracen reconquest of the Holy Land soon deprived the Teutonic Order of its original vocation and obliged its Knights to seek

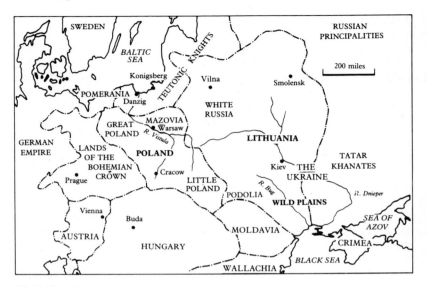

Poland and Lithuania c. 1386

fresh fields of crusading activity. By the early thirteenth century, the Order had established itself on the Baltic shore, where it might henceforward devote itself to the forcible conversion of the Prussians and Lithuanians. In the main, the Order was made up (as its name suggests) of German noblemen. However, since a spell of service with the Knights was regarded as essential training for the military life, warriors from all over Europe (Chaucer's Knight in the *Canterbury Tales*, for example) joined the Order on campaign.

The Lithuanians, who stuck obstinately to their pagan religion, were the main target of the Order's crusading expeditions. As the Knights pressed hard against their enemy, the Lithuanians turned their expansionist drive inland and southwards. Claiming that 'All Russia should belong to the Lithuanians', the Grand Duke Olgerd tore into the Russian territories presently held by the Mongol–Tatars. In 1362, at the Battle of the Blue Waters, Olgerd smashed the army fielded by the Khan and the next year, the Lithuanians took Kiev. They did not cease their advance until they had overrun the Ukraine even as far as the shores of the Black Sea.

During the reign of Grand Duke Jogaila (1382–1434), Lithuania became the largest state in Europe, occupying a territory greater than the Holy Roman Empire and three times the size of medieval France. However, the rapidity of its growth fundamentally altered the composition of the Lithuanian state. Although a pagan Grand Duke and warrior élite continued to retain power in the capital of Vilna, the lands recently added to Lithuania were predominantly Christian and populated by Russians. Furthermore, for all its meteoric rise to greatness, the Lithuanian state was a fragile creation. As it was, it lacked an effective administration and exerted little real authority over much of the land under its sway. Under pressure from the Knights, Lithuania might have as speedily dissolved as the old Kievan Russian state had done two centuries before.

Jogaila, Grand Duke of Lithuania, recognised only too well the inevitability of conversion. The majority of his subjects were now Christian and his most fearsome foe, the Teutonic Knights, claimed no other object than the subjugation of the Lithuanians to the Cross. Throughout the fourteenth century, however, the Knights had been waging war not just against Lithuania but against Poland as well, some of the territories of which they claimed for themselves. A partnership between Poland and Lithuania against the Knights was thus a possibility and might serve to restrain the Order's expansion. Evidently though, such an arrangement would be conditional upon Jogaila's conversion, for the Poles would never agree to an alliance with a pagan ruler. In order to resolve Lithuania's internal difficulties, and to preserve its independence against the Teutonic Knights, Jogaila felt bound therefore to accept Christian baptism.

* Jogaila was bold enough, however, to set terms on his own conversion. In 1385 Lithuanian envoys journeyed to Cracow in Poland where they discussed affairs of state and of religion with the leading Polish noblemen. The treaty which resulted from these talks was remarkable both in its contents and in its consequences. In return for Jogaila and his subjects accepting Christianity, the Lithuanian envoys won not only a political alliance with Poland, but the promise also that their Grand Duke would wed the Polish queen, the 10 year old Jadwiga, and become Poland's new king. Thus it came to pass. Early the next year, Jogaila was baptised and christened Wladyslaw. Three days later, he married the tiny queen, and shortly afterwards was elected and crowned King of Poland. Thus, within the space of a few months, Poland and Lithuania were joined in a dynastic union, and the Polish crown passed to the House of Jogaila or, as it was known in Poland, of Jagiellon.

The motives of the Polish lords who agreed to this extraordinary arrangement, are easily explained. With an infant girl on the throne, Poland faced the prospect of grave internal dissension. Additionally, the relentless drive of the Teutonic Knights threatened the kingdom's own borders. Already, the Knights had seized much of Pomerania and were impeding Poland's access to the Baltic along the Vistula river. An alliance with Lithuania, together with the adoption of an experienced ruler as king, might – so the Polish nobles reckoned – preserve the kingdom's strength against the forces of disaster at home and abroad.

The nobility of Poland extracted a price of its own for accepting Jogaila as king. In return for their compliance, the nobles received recognition of their right to elect the sovereign and to have him take their advice in all public matters. Early on in the next century, the leading Polish and Lithuanian lords joined themselves together into a single 'estate' or brotherhood so that they might henceforward apply a concerted pressure on the king. From the very outset, therefore, the House of Jagiellon found its authority circumscribed. Against the combined force of the nobility or *szlachta* of Poland and Lithuania, the Polish monarchy was increasingly powerless.

* By the early years of the fifteenth century, the seeds of the territorial conflicts of the early modern period had been planted. In the union of Poland and Lithuania, a vast state had been created on the eastern edge of Catholic Europe. However, Poland–Lithuania lacked a powerful monarchy capable of ordering the spread of lands which belonged to it. Political power had begun to be shared between king and nobles. This circumstance would eventually lead to the paralysis of government and to the enfeeblement of the kingdom. By contrast, in the Russian lands, a medley of states and principalities had been formed after the fall of the Kievan state. However, as a consequence of Byzantine and Mongol–Tatar influences, new notions of statehood and sovereignty were developing in Russia which concentrated political authority in the hands of the ruler. Between Poland and Russia lay the Teutonic Knights and, farther south, the expanses of forest and steppeland, variously claimed by the Tatars and Lithuanians. The contests of the sixteenth, seventeenth, and eighteenth centuries would be fought out in this middle ground set between the Baltic and the Black Seas, and between Poland–Lithuania and the newly-emergent Russian principality of Muscovy. The prize would eventually go to the state with the most effective political organization and with the greatest degree of internal cohesion.

Making Notes on 'Background'

The aim of this chapter is to acquaint you with the geographical and historical background to the period you are studying. As you read this chapter, you should concentrate on understanding what is written, rather than on making extensive notes. A couple of pages of headings with brief notes will suffice at this stage. However, it is important that you get your bearings by checking place names on the maps provided. The world of medieval eastern Europe can be confusing. The passage of time has wrought dramatic changes to the region, and today's political

boundaries bear little relation to those in existence during the middle
ages.

In making your notes, copy down the following headings. After each
one, write down a few words encapsulating what you consider to be the
most important points made in relation to the heading. After 'Landscape' (1.1.), you might choose to write, for example, 'wide, flat,
continental climate, colder in the east'.

1.   Land and climate
1.1. Landscape
1.2. Poland
1.3. The Ukraine
1.4. The forest region
2.   The Dark Ages
2.1. The Slavs
2.2. Polania–Poland
2.3. The Varangians and Russia
3.   Kievan Russia and its neighbours
3.1. Russian Christianity
3.2. The Byzantine legacy: theocratic kingship
3.3. Fragmentation
3.4. The decline of Kievan Russia
4.   The Mongol–Tatar inheritance
4.1. The conquest of Russia
4.2. Mongol–Tatar lordship
5.   Poland, Lithuania and the Teutonic Knights
5.1. Poland and Russia
5.2. The Lithuanians
5.3. The Teutonic Knights
5.4. The Polish–Lithuanian union
5.5. Future conflicts

CHAPTER 2

Expansion and Conflict

1 The Rise of Muscovy

Moscow's domination of European and, eventually, of much of Asiatic Russia could not have been foreseen in the late thirteenth century. At that time, the principality of Muscovy was shut up in the forests of the north and was only one of a dozen petty states subject to the Mongol–Tatar Khan. Yet by the early 1580s, Muscovy's dominions stretched from the Urals and Siberia westwards to the Baltic and the White Sea and, southwards, to the Caspian Sea. The reasons for this remarkable transformation will be considered in this and the following sections.

If we analyse Moscow's geographical position, three distinctive advantages appear. Firstly, Moscow lies on the river of the same name, which in turn flows into the Oka and thence into the Volga. Additionally, the upper reaches of the Oka and Volga lie close to the Dvina and Dnieper waterways which lead in turn to the Baltic and the Black Sea. Thus although it was enclosed by trackless forests, Moscow lay at the centre of a river system connecting it with the trading emporia and civilizations of southern Asia and north-east Europe. Secondly, although Moscow is situated among deciduous and evergreen forests, it stands beside a pocket of fertile soil. This tract of land, 4000 square kilometres in extent, provided the agricultural reservoir which sustained the city and its population. Thirdly, Moscow's position among the forests of the north ensured her a measure of protection from the nomadic tribes of central Asia. During the thirteenth and fourteenth centuries, therefore, Moscow provided a refuge for many former inhabitants of the more exposed Kiev region.

  * Although Moscow drew certain benefits from her geographical position, her neighbours were by no means disadvantaged. North-west of Moscow lay the city and inland port of Novgorod. Novgorod, with a population of about 20000, practised a lively trade with Scandinavia and north Germany and was a centre of manufacture. Its colonies stretched to the Urals, providing the city's merchants with a valuable supply of pelts and furs. To the west of Moscow lay Lithuania which during the fourteenth century expanded into White Russia and began encroaching massively upon Tatar territory. Bordering Moscow was the principality of Tver, whose ruler claimed the title of Grand Prince and considered himself pre-eminent among Russian rulers.

In the two centuries following the Mongol–Tatar invasion, the princes of Muscovy fought to establish their primacy in the north-west.

Tver was Moscow's earliest and closest challenge. In a series of campaigns fought during the first decades of the fourteenth century, Tver's power was broken. Henceforward, the title of Grand Prince, claimed by the rulers of Tver, was held almost continually by the princes of Moscow. The title, although it conferred neither lands nor riches, lent an impression of authority to the Muscovite ruling house and sanctioned further expansion.

* Most historians would agree that the expansion of Muscovy in the fourteenth and fifteenth centuries owed much to the abilities of the Grand Princes. On the whole, their policies were cautious and opportunistic. They did not launch ambitious wars which might have exposed the fledgling state to the danger of defeat and partition. Money, marriage and diplomatic manoeuvre were their preferred weapons, while more troublesome rivals were weakened and absorbed over a period of decades.

The caution of Moscow's early rulers is exemplified in their dealings with the Mongol–Tatars. The title of Grand Prince lay technically within the gift of the Khan. In return for granting the title, with its implied claim to primacy over the other Russian princes, the Khan expected military support and a regular flow of tribute. The princes of Muscovy took care to deliver both, and they received in turn help against their own rivals. Additionally, by acting as tribute-collectors in north-west Russia, the Grand Princes were able to divert a substantial fortune into their own coffers which they subsequently put towards the purchase of fresh land. Only in the second half of the fifteenth century did the rulers of Muscovy abandon their policy of co-operation with the Tatars.

The rulers of Muscovy further contributed to the strengthening of the state by establishing a fixed order of succession. In place of partible inheritance, the Grand Princes introduced over the fourteenth and fifteenth centuries a system of primogeniture. According to the new arrangement, the eldest son received both the lion's share of his father's properties and the princely title. Given the Russian tradition of equal inheritance, primogeniture took time to become established. Nevertheless, by arranging the enthronement of the eldest son while the father still lived, and by handing over in advance to him the majority of princely lands, the rulers of Muscovy were able to prevent the subdivision of the principality.

* Although the abilities of Moscow's early rulers may explain why they were successful in extending their territories, it remains yet to be seen why they should have wished to expand their territories at all. In a sense the answer is obvious: territorial expansion was undertaken for the sake of territory. In any agricultural society, land, power and wealth tend to be synonymous. Thus, in the middle ages the conquest of fresh lands seemed as natural and desirable as does economic growth in modern states and societies.

In Muscovy, however, the expansionist drive was nurtured by quite unique circumstances. Despite the partition of Kievan Russia in the twelfth century and its subsequent destruction by the Mongol–Tatars, the office of Grand Prince remained. As we have seen, the title of Grand Prince was taken in the early fourteenth century by the rulers of Muscovy. By virtue of this title, the princes of Muscovy claimed dominion over all the lands pertaining to the historic Kievan state. In the parlance of the age, they presumed 'sovereignty' over 'All Russia'. It was on this basis that Ivan III (1462–1505) fought the Lithuanians, arguing that they had usurped territories which belonged rightfully to him. As Ivan III put it, 'It is known that all the Russian land is by God's will our patrimony and has been since olden days, since our fore-fathers'. As he went on to explain, by 'Russian land' he meant not only the territories of Kiev and Smolensk, but also 'all the Russian lands of old'.

The orthodox faith sustained the commitment of the Muscovite princes and reinforced their expansionist ambitions. In 1326 the Metropolitan and head of the Russian orthodox church, died while visiting Moscow. The Prince convinced his successor to forsake the Metropolitan's traditional seat in Kiev and to settle permanently in Moscow. From this time on, the 'Metropolitan of Kiev and All Russia', as he named himself, remained in the city adding to Moscow's prestige. The Metropolitans claimed religious jurisdiction over all the territories which had hitherto belonged to the Kievan Russian state. By so doing, they reinforced the idea that their lay counterparts, the princes of Moscow, should themselves enjoy a claim to sovereignty over the same area.

We have already noted, in the last chapter, the impact of theology upon political belief. The Byzantine tradition of kingship was transmitted by the orthodox church into the Muscovite ideology of government. However, in 1453, the Byzantine Empire fell to the Turks, thus depriving Russian orthodoxy of its spiritual source and foundation. Muscovite commentators soon made up for the loss, arguing that since Byzantium was no more, Moscow must now be the sole repository of the true Christian religion. As Philotheos of Pskov went on to explain to Basil III:

1 And if thou rulest thine empire rightly, thou wilt be the son of light and citizen of the heavenly Jerusalem, as I have written to thee. And now I say unto thee: take care and take heed, pious Tsar: all the empires of Christendom are united in thine, for two
5 Romes have fallen and the third exists and there will not be a fourth; thy Christian empire, according to the great theologian, will not pass to others . . .

Certainly, the doctrine of the 'Third Rome', according to which

Muscovy was successor to both the Roman and Byzantine Empires, emerged in a mature form only in the sixteenth century. Even then, few took the theory literally. Nevertheless, the belief that the Muscovite ruler was in some way 'lord of orthodox Christians in the entire universe' and 'guardian of true belief' held a powerful fascination. Notions of an imperial, religious mission and destiny began therefore to take root in Moscow. During Ivan III's reign, the title of 'Caesar' or 'Tsar', meaning emperor, began to be commonly employed in court ceremonial, as indeed did the old Byzantine symbol of the double-headed eagle. The growing association with Byzantium was strengthened by Ivan III's marriage in 1472 to Sophia Paleaologus, the niece of the last Byzantine Emperor. The new prestige attaching to Muscovy eventually led in 1589 to the Metropolitan of Moscow being given the title of patriarch, a dignity which put him on the same level as the head of the Greek church in Constantinople.

2 Ivan III (1462–1505) and Basil III (1505–33)

During the reigns of Ivan III and Basil III the Muscovite state exploded outwards, and between 1462 and 1533 the territories belonging to the principality trebled in size. Behind this formidable drive to conquest lay the conjunction of forces we have identified in the preceding section: the desire to reunite the dismembered inheritance of Kievan Russia; the orthodox mission with its dynamic imperial ideology; and the basic identification of land with power. However, welding these powerful influences together was a fourth, decisive factor: the search for security. Notwithstanding its rapid expansion, the Muscovite state was still threatened by formidable neighbours. The more successful and powerful Muscovy herself became, the more it was likely that the states on her borders would collaborate together against her.

* During the second half of the fifteenth century, Lithuania presented Muscovy with her greatest political and territorial challenge. Lithuania's possessions stretched across White Russia, Smolensk and the Ukraine, barring Muscovy's expansion westwards and threatening her frontiers. Lithuania's occupation of lands which had once belonged to the Kievan Russian state and which still contained a substantial orthodox population aggravated relations with Moscow. By virtue of their inheritance and descent from the princes of Kiev, the Grand Princes believed themselves to have exclusive right to the territories held by the Lithuanians and they fiercely contested Lithuanian claims to primacy in the region. In order to counteract Muscovite ambitions, the Grand Dukes of Lithuania sought alliances with Muscovy's neighbours and endeavoured in their foreign policy to hem in their rival.

The Grand Princes Ivan III and Basil III made the defeat of the Lithuanians the major object of their foreign policy. Nevertheless, they pursued their goal with the caution typical of their predecessors. Thus

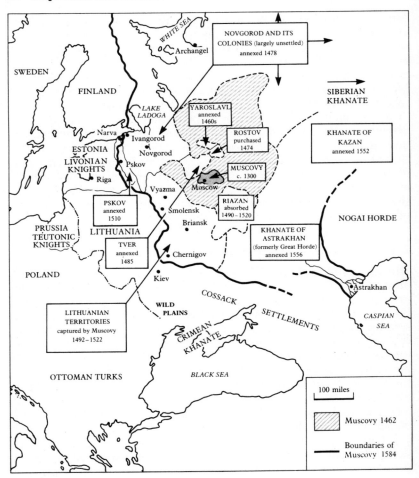

The growth of Muscovy

before commencing the war with the Lithuanians, Ivan III took care either to neutralize or to eliminate his enemy's allies. Only when this secondary object had been achieved, did he commence his war in the west.

★ At the time of Ivan's accession, the territorial unity of the Muscovite state was incomplete. In the very midst of the Grand Prince's lands lay the semi-independent principalities of Yaroslavl and Rostov. On the edge of Muscovy lay the dukedoms of Tver and Riazan and the city-states of Novgorod and Pskov. All of these were fearful of

Muscovy's growing influence in the north-west and their rulers responded favourably therefore to Lithuanian offers of friendship.

Ivan III gradually undermined the independence of his neighbours, absorbing them piecemeal and by degrees. His favourite method was to force the rulers of these states to recognise his nominal lordship and then to transform his theoretical authority into a real one over a number of years. Marriage into the ruling families, playing off one faction against the other, and outright purchase of land were alternative avenues of Ivan's diplomacy. During Ivan's reign, Yaroslavl, Rostov and Tver were thus acquired largely peacefully, with only the occasional show of force.

The skill and efficacy of Ivan's methods is exemplified in his dealings with the city of Novgorod. Although Novgorod had long recognised the Grand Prince's nominal authority, a powerful faction in the city feared that Ivan would seek to reduce the political independence of their community and make it into a satellite of Muscovy. In 1470, this faction seized power and invited Grand Duke Casimir of Lithuania to accept sovereignty over Novgorod. Ivan responded swiftly to this challenge. Before Casimir could take advantage of the offer, Ivan sent in his army. He forced the citizens to submit to him and to abandon their friendship with Duke Casimir. However, he left Novgorod's institutions of self-government largely intact and made no attempt to reduce the city's autonomy.

Gradually, once the initial crisis had passed, Ivan reduced Novgorod's political independence. In 1475 he visited the city and arrested six of its leading members. Two years later, using the excuse that the citizens were still intriguing with the Lithuanians, he again marched his army into Novgorod and abolished its institutions of government outright. Lieutenant-generals appointed by Ivan now took over the full management of affairs and Novgorod's territories were absorbed within the Grand Prince's own domain. To symbolise Novgorod's loss of independence, the bell used to summon its citizens was cut down and despatched to Moscow. Successive waves of executions and deportations robbed the vanquished inhabitants of the opportunity and will to resist.

Basil III continued the policy inaugurated by his father. In 1509–10 he turned on the city of Pskov, even though its inhabitants had been on the whole grudgingly loyal to Moscow. Pskov's leading families were deported and control of the city was given over to officials appointed by the Grand Prince. 'And these lieutenants and their agents drank much Pskovian blood', lamented the city-chronicler. Riazan suffered much the same fate. Half of its lands had already been confiscated by Muscovy during Ivan III's reign, and in 1520 Basil arrested Riazan's ruler and annexed what remained of the principality.

* During the first decades of the fifteenth century, the Tatar Golden Horde began to fall apart on account of fierce dynastic rivalries. From

the ruins of the Golden Horde, five separate warring states were established: the Great Horde (later known as the Astrakhan Khanate), the Nogai Horde, and the Crimean, Kazan and Siberian Khanates. Of these, the Great Horde posed the greatest threat to Muscovy. Its ruler, who could claim a descent going back to Ghenghis Khan, regarded the Grand Prince as his vassal and he resented Ivan's failure to pay him tribute. As a consequence, the Khan of the Great Horde proved a ready ally of the Grand Duke of Lithuania. Throughout the 1470s, the Great Horde engaged in a series of petty wars against Muscovy, egged on and abetted by the Lithuanians.

Ivan III took advantage of the rivalry between the Tatar states and established friendly relations with the Siberian and Crimean Khans. They, like he, were fearful of the Great Horde's influence and of its partnership with the Lithuanians. The success of Ivan's Tatar policy became evident in 1480. In that year, Khan Ahmed of the Great Horde joined with Casimir of Lithuania in a combined assault on Muscovy. While Ivan marched southwards against the Horde, defeating the Tatars by the River Ugra, his Crimean allies invaded Lithuania thus preventing Casimir from joining Ahmed. Shortly after his defeat by the Muscovites, Ahmed was himself attacked and slain by the Nogais, possibly acting in collusion with Ivan.

In some of the older Russian and Soviet textbooks, Ivan's 'Stand on the Ugra' is presented as the single, decisive act in the 'throwing off of the Tatar yoke'. However, most historians would now agree that Muscovy won its freedom from the Tatars gradually and that no one event marked the transition from vassalage to independence. Even as late as the middle years of the sixteenth century, rulers of Muscovy paid tribute in moments of weakness to individual Khans, thereby tacitly admitting Tatar claims to overlordship.

Ivan's relations with Kazan involved the same methods of 'divide and rule' as characterised his dealings with the other Tatar Khanates. During the 1480s Ivan took full opportunity of dynastic squabbles within the ruling house of Kazan to eliminate any threat from this quarter. By backing alternately one rival against the other, Ivan made the ruler of Kazan little more than a puppet. In this way, he was able to upset Lithuanian intrigues which had as their goal the establishment of an anti-Muscovite faction at the head of Kazan.

* By the early 1490s the overall success of Ivan III's strategy was evident. The principalities and cities neighbouring Muscovy had been brought under his direct rule. The Nogai, Kazan and Crimean Tatars had been converted into allies and the Great Horde had been humbled. The way was now clear for Ivan to start war on his chief enemy, the Grand Duke of Lithuania.

The death of the Grand Duke Casimir in 1492 and the succession of his younger son, Alexander, as ruler of Lithuania (Casimir's elder son received the crown of Poland), gave Ivan the opportunity he sought.

Taking advantage of the change of government, he launched an immediate attack on Lithuania. After a swift campaign, he compelled Alexander to hand over the province of Vyazma, and to recognise the Grand Prince of Moscow as 'Sovereign of All Russia'. By conceding this title to Ivan, Alexander effectively resigned his rights to the lands of White Russia and of the Ukraine. As a symbol of the new friendship between Lithuania and Muscovy, Alexander married Ivan's daughter, the princess Elena.

During the late 1490s relations between Muscovy and Lithuania deteriorated once more. Recognising the implications of the title 'Sovereign of All Russia', Alexander soon ceased to address Ivan in this way. Additionally, he embarked upon the persecution of orthodox believers in the Lithuanian lands, even to the extent of imprisoning his orthodox Muscovite wife. Using these insults as an excuse, Ivan took up arms once more. In 1500, his troops advanced on a wide front, overrunning the regions around Smolensk, Briansk and Chernigov (see map on page 22). The war begun by Ivan was concluded by his son and successor, Basil III, who captured the town of Smolensk in 1514. By the terms of the treaty agreed in 1522 between Basil and Grand Duke Sigismund, Muscovy retained its conquest of what amounted to over a third of the land previously occupied by the Lithuanians.

3 Ivan IV (1533–84)

When Basil III died in 1533, his son and successor, Ivan IV, was only three years old and it was not until 1547 that Ivan began to rule in deed as well as in name. In that year, Ivan was crowned 'Tsar' or Emperor of Russia by the Metropolitan of Moscow. From this point onwards, Tsar would be the official title of the Grand Princes and rulers of Russia.

Unlike his predecessors, Ivan did not make the struggle with Lithuania the principal goal of his foreign policy. Instead, he looked first of all towards the Tatar Khanates, and he spent the early part of his reign in war with Kazan and Astrakhan (the successor of the Great Horde). Once he had accomplished their defeat, Ivan switched his attention northwards to the Baltic shore and to the territories of the Livonian Knights (a branch of the Teutonic Order). The war which he fought on the Baltic was prolonged by Polish–Lithuanian and Swedish intervention, and proved ultimately futile.

Ivan's interest in the Khanates and the Baltic may be explained in various ways. In the surviving sixteenth-century accounts, the opinion most commonly given was that Ivan sought to recover his 'patrimony' and to convert 'godless saracens' and 'heretics' to the true orthodox faith. Although Ivan was doubtless inspired by this sort of imperial, crusading rhetoric, two practical considerations also influenced his foreign policy. Firstly, he was attracted by the prospect of opening up trading links with Persia and, through the Baltic, with western Europe.

Secondly, by the time of his accession, both the Tatar Khanates and Livonia were in an advanced state of disintegration. A power vacuum thus threatened which might variously draw in the Ottoman Turks, the Swedes and the Lithuanians, and so in turn endanger Muscovy's own frontiers. In order to forestall any such eventuality, Ivan had to grasp the initiative and to act first.

* By the time of Ivan's accession, the internal politics of Kazan had reached such a point of confusion as to threaten the survival of the Khanate altogether. Rival factions clashed for power, one looking to Moscow for help, the other to the Crimea and to the Crimean Khan's own ally, the Ottoman Turks. Coups and rebellions followed in rapid and bloody succession.

At first, Ivan was content to exploit Kazan's weakness by annexing its territories piecemeal. However, the imminent dissolution of the Khanate rapidly obliged Ivan to embark upon a more determined course. Accordingly, in 1552, Ivan marched on Kazan with a force of 150 000 men and 150 cannons. Using explosives, he first blew up the water supply of the city of Kazan and then breached its walls. Having gained entry, the Muscovites made a bloodbath of the defenders. Over the next few years, Ivan incorporated all that remained of the Kazan Khanate within the Muscovite state. Military governors were appointed over the region, its people were forcibly converted to orthodox Christianity, and the lands of Kazan were distributed amongst the Russian nobility. In thanks for the victory God had given him over the 'saracens', Ivan began the construction of St Basil's Cathedral in Moscow's Red Square. With its bright onion-shaped domes, St Basil's is to this day Moscow's most celebrated landmark.

Following the capture of Kazan on the middle Volga, Ivan turned his attention to the mouth of the river. Astrakhan, which was all that remained of the Great Horde, fell to the Muscovites in 1556 and was promptly annexed. As a consequence of the capture of Astrakhan, the entire course of the Volga River down to the Caspian Sea passed into Muscovy's possession. Russian merchants were therefore now able to trade directly with the centres of silk production in Persia and the Middle East. Nevertheless, despite this new opportunity, Ivan's interest lay less with the emporia of the Orient than with the cities of Europe. The Tsar's desire to facilitate mercantile links with the west led him to establish diplomatic and commercial relations with England and, later on, to engage in a costly and fruitless war.

* Even during the reign of Ivan III there had been a growing commercial traffic between Muscovy and the Baltic region. German merchants were frequent visitors to the city of Novgorod, and Muscovy's capture of this port had opened up new opportunities for commerce between its interior and western Europe. In the 1490s Ivan III had constructed a new port at Ivangorod on the Baltic to facilitate this trade. However, owing to the close proximity of the Livonian

commercial centre of Narva, Ivangorod failed to prosper.

In 1553 the English merchant and navigator, Richard Chancellor arrived in the White Sea by ship. Chancellor had been searching for a passage to China over the northern tip of Scandinavia. However, storms and ice obliged him to halt his expedition and to put to shore near Archangel. To his surprise, since he had no idea where he was, Chancellor was greeted by subjects of the Tsar, who forthwith bore him off to their master. Ivan's interest in the visitor was immediate and soon resulted in diplomatic and commercial links being established with England. In 1555 Ivan granted the Muscovy Company, set up in London after Chancellor's return, the right to trade freely throughout his dominions.

The developing trade with England not only gave Ivan access to the technical products which his country lacked, but also offered new diplomatic opportunities. During the late 1560s he attempted, on the basis of his good relations with England, to draw Queen Elizabeth into an offensive alliance against Poland. Although the plan came to nought, it was sufficient to arouse the concern of the Polish sovereign. England's interest in Muscovy derived from the supply of furs which might be bought there and in the opportunities for commercial expansion along the Volga towards Persia.

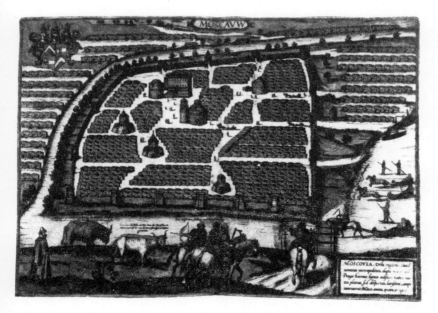

Moscow in the sixteenth century. Engraving from Braun und Hohenburg, Orbis Terrarum, 1570

The principal obstacle to Russia's trading and diplomatic relations with England and with Europe as a whole, lay in her lack of convenient ports. The main *entrepôt* for Anglo–Russian trade was Archangel. Archangel, however, was ice-bound for six months of the year and could only be reached by foreign merchants after a dangerous passage through the Arctic. Additionally, since Archangel was located some 700 miles north of Moscow, it was less than ideal for native traders. By contrast, the Baltic ports were open for most of the year, were closer to Muscovy's principal commercial centres, and were already well established as trading communities. Furthermore, with Livonia in decline, the ports of Narva, Reval and Riga might, so Ivan reckoned, be obtained with relative ease. The catch was that not only Muscovy had an interest in the Baltic commerce and in the fate of Livonia, but Sweden and Poland–Lithuania as well.

* Livonia had been the first of the crusading states on the Baltic and had been set up by the Order of Swordbearers. During the thirteenth century, the Livonians had joined with the Teutonic Order and had co-operated in campaigns against the Order's various neighbours. Nevertheless, despite their merger, the Livonian Knights had preserved their own institutions, cornering much of the Baltic trade and engaging in private wars against Novgorod and Pskov. In 1525, the Grand Master of the Teutonic Knights converted to Lutheranism and transformed the Teutonic Order into the state of Prussia. The Livonians were therefore left as Europe's last crusading colony. Isolation was followed by disintegration. Many of the Livonian Knights embraced Protestantism and gave up their life in the barracks for a quieter existence as rural proprietors. From their manor houses, they organized the work of their Latvian and Estonian peasants and engaged in their petty feuds. Attempts by the Master of the Order and the Archbishop of Riga to preserve Livonian unity were soon lost in their own squabbles.

Taking advantage of Livonia's internal difficulties, Ivan invaded the country in 1558. At this point, the Livonian state and military order finally fell apart. Its last master handed over the Order's lands to Poland in return for receiving Courland as a hereditary duchy. The cities of the north, led by Reval, meanwhile placed themselves under Swedish protection. Thus, at the height of his victory in Livonia, Ivan found himself at war simultaneously with the two greatest Baltic powers. For the next 20 years, Ivan was to be engaged in a hopeless struggle to preserve his Livonian conquests and to win his 'window on the west'.

Ivan's fight to maintain his hold over Livonia was almost certain to be a failure. In order to retain an outlet to the Baltic, Ivan was ready to make concessions and enter into alliances. Thus, he did not demand the entirety of Livonia or even full sovereignty over the part he claimed. Indeed, he was ready to negotiate even to the extent of supporting the candidacy of a Danish puppet to the Livonian 'crown'. However, year

Muscovy and the Lands About

The province of *Moscow* is not overextensive or fertile, for the sandy soil which covers it and which kills the corn with the least excess of dryness of moisture, is a great obstacle to fertility. To this must be added the immoderate and excessive inclemency of the atmosphere, for the cold is sometimes so intense that the earth splits into clefts and water thrown in the air freezes before it reaches the ground . . . The city itself is built of wood and tolerably larger than it really is, for the gardens and spacious courtyards in every house make a great addition to the city . . . They say that six years before my arrival at Moscow, the houses were counted by an order of the prince and that the number exceeded 41 500. The city is broad and spacious and very dirty.

An early sixteenth-century German observer

They report that the grass here in the *Ukraine* generally grows so high that a man on horseback is easily hid under it. The country abounds with all sorts of grain, that the inhabitants know not what to do with it . . . They have also all sorts of beast, fish and fowl . . .

A seventeenth-century Irish traveller

The bishops and the *Livonian Order* have almost no fortresses . . . and no one builds anything here for defence. In the same way, the common nobility is provided with no fortresses whatsoever, but only with open farms . . . The three cities, however, Riga, Reval and Dorpat, have a fine trade and a merchant guild in which sit rather rich and wealthy burghers . . . If everyone fulfilled the service imposed upon him, they would have altogether some 6000 horses. Since time out of mind, however, almost no mustering has been either seen or held.

A Swedish report on Livonia, c. 1550

The *Siberian land* lies towards the north-eastern regions, a great distance from Moscow . . . On the Ural mountains grow cedars, pines and others; and among them deer, elk, hare, fox, sable, glutton and squirrel have their dwelling places. From this range, many rivers issue, vast and beautiful rivers, and in them the freshest waters and an abundance of various fishes.

A seventeenth-century Muscovite account

after year, the Muscovites were beaten back. By 1581, the Polish army of King Stephen Bathory lay before Pskov and Ivan had lost the city of Ivangorod to the Swedes. Eventually at the peace of Yam Zapolski (1582), Bathory compelled Ivan to renounce his rights to Livonia and to give up his struggle for a port on the Baltic shore. The next year, Ivan finally surrendered the coastline of the Gulf of Finland to the Swedes. The desperate military plight of Russia during these years of struggle is suggested by the ease with which Tatar raiders penetrated into the heart of Ivan's lands. In 1571, a Crimean army succeeded in setting fire to part of the capital. A Tatar expedition launched two years later was halted only 50 miles from Moscow.

   * Ivan's defeat and humiliation in Livonia occurred simultaneously with the conquest and opening up of Siberia. The capture of Novgorod by Ivan III had brought under Muscovy's sway the city's colonies and trading outposts which extended to the Ural mountains. The annexation of Kazan by Ivan IV additionally extended the Russian frontier eastwards to the point where it adjoined Siberia. Ivan entrusted the task of penetrating into the Siberian territories to the merchant family of Stroganov. In 1574 the Stroganovs were granted the concession by Ivan to settle the lands east of the Urals and to seize whatever commercial benefit they could from the area.

   Since the middle of the fifteenth century, Siberia had belonged to the Tatar Khan who resided in the city of Sibir. At the beginning of Ivan IV's reign, Khan Yediger of Siberia had recognised the Tsar's suzerainty and had paid him tribute. Yediger, however, was later deposed by a rival, Khan Kuchum, who forthwith ceased payments to Moscow. In view of the evident hostility of the Siberian ruler, the Stroganovs were obliged to furnish a military expedition to support their ambitions in the region. Around 1580 they enlisted the aid of the Cossack warrior, Yermak. With only a few hundred men, Yermak crossed the Urals and defeated Kuchum, occupying his capital.

   Yermak was slain in 1585 in the continuing struggle with the Tatars for the Siberian lands. Nevertheless, his victory over Kuchum opened up the Ob and Irtysch rivers, which subsequently became the highways of Russian settlement in Siberia. In the wake of the Stroganovs' colonisation of the territory east of the Urals, came military governors who rapidly made the region subject to the direct control of the Tsar. However, although Ivan did not live to see these later developments, they would have yielded him little comfort. His main concern was to open up a passage to the Baltic and to western Europe, not to enter upon a new inheritance in distant Asia.

4 The Union of Lublin (1569)

The union of Poland and Lithuania was personal in origin and had its roots in the marriage of Queen Jadwiga to the Grand Duke Jogaila in

1386 (see page 15). In the centuries which followed, the connection between the two countries was strengthened until in 1569 it was declared indissoluble. In the Union of Lublin, sealed that year, both countries merged together to make a single political unit known as the Polish Commonwealth. It was in this form that Poland and Lithuania were to continue their shared existence until the close of the eighteenth century.

Poland's long connection with Lithuania, cemented at Lublin in 1569, was remarkable given the many differences between the two countries. Poland was a long-established feudal monarchy. It had a social order based on estates; representative institutions; a powerful nobility well versed in its rights; and a coherent system of administration and justice. Although by no means homogeneous in terms of population and religious affiliation (there were extensive areas of German settlement in the towns, as well as large pockets of Jews, Armenians and Ukrainians), the leading noblemen both in the court and in the provinces were overwhelmingly Catholic and of Polish extraction.

By contrast, Lithuania was a new creation, born of the sudden rush of Lithuanian tribes into the lands of western Russia. In much of the area they had conquered, the Lithuanians had left the local rulers in place and had preserved the existing laws and customs intact. A medley of jurisdictions and procedures thus persisted, defying attempts at centralisation. In its ethnic and religious composition, Lithuania was similarly diverse. Lithuanians made up only a quarter of the duchy's inhabitants, the majority being Russians and Ukrainians. The orthodox faith continued to attract the greatest number of believers, despite Catholic attempts at conversion.

Since its connection with Poland was personal and dynastic, Lithuania continued until 1569 to have its own government. A Grand Ducal Council, meeting in the capital of Vilna, ordered both the duchy's internal affairs and its foreign policy. So as to placate the leading noblemen of Lithuania, the King of Poland was often obliged to renounce his title of Grand Duke and to appoint a relative to this office. The potential for a dissolution of the union was never greater than on these occasions.

* Throughout the period 1386–1569 a gradual process of 'polonisation' took place in Lithuania which eliminated differences and established a community of interests. In 1413 the leading Lithuanian lords were 'adopted' by their Polish counterparts and given the same privileges as the Polish nobility. Polish forms of government, of law, and of social organization were henceforward assumed in Lithuania. The Catholic church and the newly-established university of Vilna acted additionally as powerful agents of Polish cultural diffusion.

Jogaila's marriage to Jadwiga in 1386 had been inspired by a fear, common to Poles and Lithuanians alike, of the Teutonic Knights. The persistent threat of invasion from the Knights served to drive Poland and Lithuania ever closer. It was not until 1466 that the military power of the Order was broken by the combined armies of its Polish and Lithuanian rivals and by a rebellion of its subjects. The final stage in the Order's history came in 1525 when its Grand Master, Albert Hohenzollern, embraced Lutheranism and made the new Protestant Duchy of Prussia a fief of the Polish crown.

The 'German menace' was rapidly replaced by a new threat. The Jagiellon family had its first unhappy experience with the Ottoman Turks in 1444. In that year, Wladyslaw III of Poland, who had previously been elected King of Hungary, was killed by the Turks at the Battle of Varna. From the Balkans, the Ottomans regularly launched raids into Polish and Lithuanian territory. In the second half of the fifteenth century, the Turks also established themselves on the Black Sea coast, overrunning the Lithuanian territories around the mouth of the Dnieper River. All attempts to recapture the coastline had to be abandoned in the 1520s, when the Turkish conquest of Hungary opened up a new threat on Poland's southern frontier. By this time, of course, Lithuania was also at war with Muscovy and had already lost a third of its territory to its eastern neighbour.

* The danger posed by Ivan IV's vigorous expansion occurred simultaneously with a crisis in the Jagiellon monarchy. Sigismund Augustus, the elderly King of Poland and Grand Duke of Lithuania, was heirless. Since he was the last of the Jagiellon line the union of Poland and Lithuania would automatically dissolve on his death. Dilatory discussions concerning a closer union between the two countries had been in progress for some decades. Now, under the combined impact of the Muscovite challenge and the King's impending death, the nobility of Lithuania demanded full unity with Poland: 'one common lord and one common defence'.

The concern of the Lithuanian nobility to merge their state with Poland is understandable. Lithuania was bearing the brunt of the Muscovite advance and was, by itself, incapable of prolonged resistance. Its army depended upon Polish troops and resources; its towns and countryside were already exhausted by the heavy tax burden needed to continue the fighting. Full union would facilitate Lithuania's defence by providing easier access to Polish arms and cash.

For its part, the Polish nobility saw Lithuania as providing new opportunities for land acquisition. At a time when the countries of western Europe were planting overseas colonies, the Poles were seeking new areas of settlement for themselves in the east. A merger of Poland and Lithuania would, so the Polish nobles calculated, remove many of the obstacles to colonization.

Discussions over the terms of Poland's union with Lithuania were pursued with increasing urgency and eventually reached fruition in 1569. At an assembly made up of representatives of both countries which met that year at Lublin, it was agreed to form a 'Commonwealth' (*Rzeczpospolita*) 'of two states and nations, joined together in one people, and for perpetuity a single ruler, one common lord and King, jointly elected by the Poles and Lithuanians'. The office of Grand Duke of Lithuania would henceforth be inseparable from the office of King of Poland and the parliament of Lithuania (set up in 1559 for the sole purpose of agreeing to the proposed union) would amalgamate with the parliament or *Seym* of Poland.

As an annex to the agreement worked out in Lublin, Podolia, Volhynia and the Ukraine were removed from Lithuanian administration and given over directly to Polish rule. A wave of Polish settlement descended upon these provinces, and huge estates or *latifundia* were carved out by ambitious colonists. In the next century, these large landed proprietors would exercise a disproportionate influence over the

The Polish Commonwealth

political institutions of Poland, and they would contribute significantly to the paralysis of government which affected the Polish Commonwealth. The more immediate result of Lithuania's cession of the Ukraine was, however, to bring Poland into direct contact with a new and dangerous element: the Cossacks of the western steppe.

5 The Cossacks

The Ukraine is the name usually employed nowadays to designate the homeland of the Ukrainian people. By this measure, the area of the Ukraine stretches from Lvov and Galicia in the west to the Sea of Azov in the east, while the Black Sea and the Pripet marshes mark respectively the region's southern and northern limits. These boundaries roughly coincide with those of today's Ukrainian Soviet Socialist Republic, which is one of the 15 constituent republics of the USSR. However, in the middle ages, *ukraina* meant simply 'borderland'. Only gradually did the name come to fix on a specific geographical area, populated by a distinct ethnic and linguistic group. For most of their history, therefore, the Ukrainians have been known as Ruthenians or, because they speak a variety of the Russian language, as Little Russians.

The Cossacks were a product of the *ukraina* in the original sense of the word. In the frontier steppe region of southern Russia, they performed as pioneersmen, freebooters and mercenaries. The word 'Cossack' reflects the early qualities of Cossack life. For 'Cossack' is a rendering of *kazak*, which among the Tatars meant adventurer or free-lance warrior. Indeed, the first *kazaks* were probably Tatars, fighting independently of the Khan. In the fifteenth century, however, the Cossacks were 'slavicised' by recruits drawn from neighbouring Slav communities.

The steppe zone of southern Russia, which includes the Ukraine of today, was the Cossack heartland. Cossack villages – essentially blockhouses providing accommodation in winter – were established on the Dnieper, Don and Volga rivers. From their remote camps, the Cossacks launched raiding expeditions into Lithuania and Muscovy. Additionally, they used the rivers to provide a passage for their warboats and they plundered as far south as the Turkish cities on the Black Sea coast.

The Cossacks prized their status as free warriors, being in the words of a later traveller, 'inconceivable lovers of liberty and impatient under the mildest slavery'. Each community annually elected its own leaders or Hetmans who organized campaigns, apportioned booty, and administered justice. During office, the Hetman was responsible to the warrior band, which retained the right to dismiss him at will. The Cossacks subsisted in the main by plunder, bartering for supplies with visiting merchants. To begin with, they avoided any settled activity like farming, which was held 'to bring inglory and dishonour'.

* Over the course of the sixteenth and seventeenth centuries, the Cossacks gradually lost their political and economic independence. During this time, the edges of the Polish and Muscovite states rolled across the steppeland of the Ukraine, converting border territories into areas of fixed settlement. As a 'peripheral society' and product of the frontier, the Cossacks were doomed to lose their freedom once they became incorporated within a political structure.

Since the time of the Mongol–Tatar onslaught the fertile steppeland had been only thinly populated. The open grasslands were too vulnerable to attack to make their settlement worthwhile. Most of the Ukrainian population huddled, therefore, around the few fortified towns in the region. All this changed in the sixteenth century. At this time, a worsening of labour conditions in Muscovy released a flood of refugees into the Ukraine, who rapidly established their own farmsteads and communities on the steppe. Meanwhile, the Lithuanians gradually introduced a new stability of conditions in the area under their charge. From Kiev and Braslav, campaigns were launched to impose order on the countryside, and a provincial administration was set up. In the wake of this political reorganization came a new influx of gentry and peasants.

The 'colonization' of the Ukraine was accompanied by the spread of aristocratic landholding in the region. Vast tracts of territory or *latifundia* were given away by the Kings of Poland and the Grand Dukes of Lithuania to their leading noblemen. This process gathered pace after the Union of Lublin (1569), one of the consequences of which was to throw the Ukraine open to aristocratic pioneers. As the newly-arrived 'kinglets' feudalized their *latifundia*, imposing burdensome obligations on the population, many peasants simply moved further eastwards, opening up in turn new land for colonization.

Among the Cossacks, the ordering and settlement of the Ukraine elicited a variety of responses. Some Cossacks simply entered the service of the King of Poland, and in return for 'registration' received the promise of regular employment as border guards. Others joined in the work of settlement and established themselves as Cossack landowners and serf-masters. However, many Cossacks refused to give up their old way of life. At first, they endeavoured to prolong their marauding, regardless of the tide of settlement and conquest. Vigorous campaigning by the Polish army, culminating in the Cossack defeat at Lubny in 1596, revealed the hopelessness of this course. With no alternative left to them, many Cossacks moved eastwards, beyond the area of colonization. Accordingly, they occupied the Wild Plains, the unsettled territory on the lower Dnieper, and established their headquarters at Zaporozhe. By the 1590s, the 'Zaporozhian Host' numbered 20000 warriors, organized under their own elected leaders. By pursuing an independent foreign policy and raiding deep into the Ottoman Empire and the Commonwealth, the Cossack Zaporozhian Host soon constituted a power in its own right on the farthest edge of eastern Europe.

Making notes on 'Expansion and Conflict'

This chapter is principally concerned with the growth of the principality of Muscovy in the period of the fifteenth and sixteenth centuries. The final two sections deal respectively with territorial changes affecting Poland and Lithuania over the same period, and with the birth of 'Cossackdom' in the Ukraine.

The chapter covers both a wide geographical area and an extended time-span. However, it is broken up into manageable sections as an aid to understanding and to making notes. As you read, you should think in particular not just about *what* happened but *why* it happened as well. Why, therefore, did the princes of Muscovy seek to expand their territories? Why was Muscovy so successful? Why did Poland and Lithuania formalize their union and merge together in 1569? Why did the Cossacks set up as an independent force in the Ukraine and resist attempts at their absorption? The following headings, sub-headings and tasks may help you to make notes:

1.   The rise of Muscovy
1.1. Geographical advantages
1.2. Muscovy's neighbours: Novgorod and Tver; Tatars and Lithuanians
1.3. The work of the Grand Princes
In what ways might the rise of Muscovy be considered unexpected? Where did Muscovy's special strengths lie?
1.4. Motives for expansion. This last section provides you with a basis upon which to identify the motives of Ivan III, Basil III and Ivan IV. As you read the sections which follow, think in particular about how a sense of religious and historic obligation may have influenced the rulers of Muscovy.
2.   Ivan III and Basil III
2.1. Aims
2.2. The Lithuanian menace
2.3. Muscovy's conquest of her neighbours
2.4. The Tatars
2.5. The Lithuanian War. What factors prevented Ivan III from making war on Lithuania as soon as he became the ruler of Muscovy?
3.   Ivan IV
3.1. Aims. What was the significance of Ivan IV taking the title of 'Tsar'?

3.2. Kazan and Astrakhan
3.3. Trade and commerce
3.4. The Livonian War
3.5. Siberia
How many of Ivan's aims had been met by the close of his reign? Do you consider his foreign policy to have been a success or a failure?
4.   The Union of Lublin
4.1. Poland and Lithuania: contrasts
4.2. Polonisation and foreign threats
4.3. The dynastic crisis and the Union of Lublin
Many historians have presented the Union of Lublin as the necessary consequence of the 1386 marriage of Jogaila to Jadwiga. Do you consider the Union of Lublin to have been in any way inevitable, or was it instead the product of a quite unexpected series of events?
5.   The Cossacks
5.1. Cossack origins
5.2. The settlement of the Ukraine
In what sense were the Cossacks a 'phenomenon of the frontier'? With what other groups and societies known to you, do they share certain common characteristics?

Answering essay questions on 'Expansion and Conflict'

Questions on the growth of Muscovy are occasional visitors to A-level papers. Because Russia is often regarded as an 'unpopular' topic, the questions set are for the most part simply stated and they invite a straightforward response. A typical question might be:

> 'Account for the rapid territorial growth of the state of Muscovy during the fifteenth and sixteenth centuries.'

In tackling this question, remember that 'account for' does not mean the same as 'give an account of'. 'Account for' is another way of saying 'explain'; accordingly, your essay should be an explanation, not an outline of events. In preparing your answer, first construct a brief plan. Start your plan by arranging the title so as to provide you with a structure for your essay. In place of the title, write:

> 'One explanation for the rapid growth of the state of Muscovy during the fifteenth and sixteenth centuries is . . .'

Under this heading, you should now compose a series of brief statements which seem to follow on. You might choose to write, for instance:

the abilities of her rulers
the weakness of her enemies
the sense of religious and historical mission.

These statements will provide you with a framework around which to draft your paragraphs. When it comes to writing, expand each with concrete examples. Under 'the abilities of her rulers', you might choose to discuss Ivan III's caution and consistency of purpose, or Ivan IV's opportunism as demonstrated by his wars against the Khanates and Livonia.

In writing your conclusion, make it absolutely clear to the reader what your overall explanation is. It is quite sufficient to state, bald though it may appear, 'The rapid territorial growth of Muscovy may thus be accounted for by the abilities of her rulers, the weakness of her enemies, etc.'.

Source-based questions on 'Expansion and Conflict'

1 The Third Rome
Read the extract taken from the letter of Philotheos of Pskov, given on page 20, and answer the following questions:
a) Explain the term 'Tsar'. Whence did this term derive?
b) Identify the second and third Romes.
c) What does this extract tell us about the way some orthodox churchmen perceived Muscovy's role in international affairs?

2 Muscovy and the Lands About
Read the four extracts describing the province of Muscovy, the Ukraine, the lands of the Livonian Order and Siberia on page 29. Look also at the illustration on page 27. Answer the following questions:
a) To what extent is the written description of the city of Moscow confirmed by the evidence of the contemporary illustration?
b) Using the evidence of the sources, explain how the limitations of geography and climate experienced in Muscovy might have encouraged the principality's expansion into the lands of its neighbours.
c) According to the Swedish report, what factors made Livonia particularly vulnerable to foreign attack?
d) Using the evidence given in these sources and any other information known to you, outline the reasons for and the results of Ivan IV's decision to conquer Livonia.

CHAPTER 3

Government and Politics

1 Chanceries and *Pomeshchiki*

During the late fifteenth and sixteenth centuries, the social and political structure of the Muscovite state was drastically reshaped by the policies of its rulers. Under the direction of Ivan III and Basil III, new systems of government and of administration were established in place of the rudimentary institutions inherited from the middle ages. At the same time, a new class of warriors was created and brought into the service of the ruler. These important changes were largely the consequence of Muscovy's rapid territorial growth, which exposed the deficiencies of its existing administrative institutions and the weaknesses of its system of military provision.

During the middle ages, the work of government in Muscovy was divided between two groups of people. More important matters, such as advising the Prince on policy, mustering troops, and maintaining control in the provinces, were undertaken by the boyars. These comprised the ruler's most trusted associates and usually consisted of the larger landowners. More routine administrative tasks, such as preparing lists of taxpayers, were undertaken by the *dvor* or household, which was made up of the Prince's private palace staff. Overall the whole business of running Muscovy lay until the late fifteenth century in the hands of probably no more than two dozen people.

During the last decades of the fifteenth century, Muscovy was rapidly transformed from a petty principality to the largest state in Europe. The rudimentary administrative methods worked out in the middle ages were plainly no longer suitable for a state with a population of six million and with a landmass of about 600 000 square miles. In order to communicate over long distances and to gather information and resources across a wide geographical area, the Prince stood in urgent need of a larger and more efficient apparatus of government.

Ivan III's initial response to Muscovy's changed administrative needs was simply to increase the size of his household staff by admitting to its ranks a corps of literate officials. By the close of his reign there were about 50 of these *diaki* or secretaries working in the household. Their principal task was the drafting of correspondence and the maintenance of public records.

The complexity of governmental operations caused by the continued growth of the state soon obliged a more radical remodelling of the administration. During the first decades of the sixteenth century, a number of departments were set up within the household and each was given special responsibility for a single activity of government. By the middle years of the century, many of these departments had acquired sufficient status and importance to be placed outside the household service altogether. These chanceries or *prikazy*, as they were known, were directly responsible to the Prince and they served as centres of specialist expertise and knowledge. The emergence of these new units of government, with their teams of experienced secretaries and well defined procedures, is commonly perceived by historians as marking the first stage in the development of the Muscovite bureaucracy.

* The extension of the household administration and the establishment of the first chanceries was not accompanied by any change in the central decision-making institutions of government. The boyars continued to advise the Prince and to participate in most of the discussions affecting important business of state. Gradually, however, their influence was undermined by the secretaries, who had a greater specialist knowledge and a more sophisticated understanding of public affairs. On several occasions in the late fifteenth century, Ivan III by-passed the boyars and sought advice at first hand from the secretaries.

During the reign of Basil III individual chanceries began to encroach further on established boyar prerogatives. Boyars had traditionally been appointed as provincial governors, fulfilling their local responsibilities with only minimal supervision. Basil, however, placed all local affairs under chancery oversight and sent out secretaries to supervise the work of the governors. Many of the duties performed by the governors, such as collecting taxes and preparing lists of warriors, were also taken over by the chancery administration. Certainly, neither Ivan nor Basil intentionally sought to diminish the prestige and status of the boyars. They were principally interested in efficiency and in obtaining a greater degree of informed and centralised direction. Nevertheless, the growth of 'secretary government' embittered the boyars and made them resentful of the new administrative practices.

* The most important function traditionally falling to the boyars was the provision of troops. At time of war, the boyars were expected to provide armed warriors drawn from their own estates. These augmented the forces gathered by the Prince from his personal or domain lands. Until the late fifteenth century, therefore, the bulk of the Muscovite army consisted of private retinues led by boyar chieftains. Since, however, the ruler had no direct influence upon the quality and quantity of troops supplied by the boyars, this system of military provision led to extreme uncertainty. On several occasions during the fifteenth century, the Muscovite army was defeated solely because individual boyars failed to assemble sufficient troops.

During the first years of Ivan's reign a reform of the system of military provision was undertaken which fundamentally reshaped Muscovite society. At Ivan's direction, many of the recently conquered territories were confiscated from their former owners and parcelled out to members of the household and to other leading Muscovites. In return for receiving these estates, the new owners were expected to provide the Prince with a fixed number of armed men at time of war. A special chancery was set up to ensure that military obligations were fulfilled and that each warrior was suitably equipped with a horse, chain-mail armour and weapons. All this had to be paid for by the landowner from the produce and profit he made out of the estate granted him. Failure to abide by these commitments rendered the estate liable to confiscation.

The new system of *pomeste* or conditional land tenure was first introduced in the Novgorod region during the 1480s and 1490s, and was rapidly extended over the rest of the country. Not only were the properties of vanquished Khans, princes and cities converted into *pomeste*-holdings, but much of the common land tilled by the peasantry was also expropriated. As a consequence of this extensive process of land distribution, there were by the middle years of the sixteenth century about 20000 *pomeshchiki* or *pomeste*-holders in Muscovy. Although ill-equipped by western standards, the *pomeshchiki* at least provided a reliable source of manpower and freed the ruler from his military dependence on the boyars.

2 The Boyars and the Minority of Ivan IV

The boyars had traditionally made up the élite of Muscovite society. They advised the Prince in person, undertook military and civil tasks at his behest, and regularly received gifts of land in return for their support. Originally, the Prince had the right to make anyone they wished a boyar and to elevate persons of even humble origin to this high status. During the fourteenth and early fifteenth centuries, however, the ranks of the boyars had become increasingly rigidified and closed to outsiders.

Sharp differences in wealth divided the leading boyar families. Some boyars, like the Shuisky family from Suzdal, owned huge freehold properties or *votchina*; others possessed only a few villages and were thus poorer than many non-boyar landowners. Differences of status also distinguished the leading families. Those boyars of a more illustrious pedigree tended to occupy the principal court offices and composed the Prince's innermost circle of advisers. Those outside this group filled positions in the provincial government. During the fifteenth and early sixteenth centuries, a hierarchy of precedence or *mestnichestvo* was worked out in Moscow which laid down firmly which families might hold which offices of state. These gradations of wealth and of honour prevented the boyars from uniting together against encroachments on their influence.

During the reign of Ivan III, the boyar élite began to lose its traditional monopoly of influence. The rise of the secretaries and chanceries challenged the boyars' power at court and the rise of the *pomeshchiki* made their private armies an increasingly redundant form of military provision. At the same time, the ranks of the boyars were suddenly thrown open to a host of newcomers. Rather than banish or execute the rulers of the principalities which he had recently annexed, Ivan III chose instead to accommodate them within the existing boyar hierarchy. By taking the social and political élite of the conquered regions into his service, Ivan hoped to unite these areas more firmly to Muscovy. By the early years of the sixteenth century, about a half of Muscovy's boyar families consisted of former princelings.

The large number of new admissions to the boyar élite deepened the sense of insecurity already felt by the older families. An intense factional rivalry was generated as individual families sought to preserve their declining influence over the ruler and to exclude their rivals from power.

Ivan III and Basil III both succeeded in containing these divisions by choosing their leading advisers from among each of the leading boyar factions and by posing as disinterested arbiters in the boyars' internal disputes. In 1533, however, Basil died and the throne passed to his son, Ivan IV. Because Ivan was only three years old at the time of his father's death, a regency was declared.

* On his deathbed, Basil had implored the boyars 'to stand firm that my son may be made sovereign of the state and so that there may be justice in the land'. The boyars had nodded their assent. However, despite their promises, the boyars rapidly took the opportunity of Basil's death to engage in vicious factional feuding. Over the next decade, a succession of families – the Belskys, Shuiskys and Glinskys – seized power in a series of palace coups. With each turn of the wheel, the victorious family executed or exiled its rivals and advanced the fortunes of its own supporters. As Ivan IV was later to comment of this period of boyar misrule: 'I was orphaned and the tsardom was a widow. And so our boyars seized the opportunity for themselves . . . and no one prohibited them from their totally unseemly undertaking'.

During their years in power, the boyar families made little attempt to weaken the apparatus of government; as the *de facto* rulers of the state they had after all little interest in doing so. Nevertheless, boyar rule led to an overall erosion in the power of central government. Individual boyars carved out extensive areas of local influence in the countryside and they allowed the system of provincial government to fall into decay. During this time, many *pomeshchiki* were encouraged to put aside the obligations which they owed to the Prince and to become instead boyar clients and service-warriors. As Andrew of Staritsa advised a group of *pomeste*-holders in 1537, 'The Grand Prince is young and the boyars hold the state, and whom have you to serve? Come to serve me and I am glad to make grants of land to you.'

Later accounts tell of how the young Ivan IV was physically

maltreated by the boyars. Although the sources for this period are notoriously few, these allegations should probably be discounted. The boyars needed Ivan's name and authority to lend credibility to their rule and, as he got older, his goodwill to stay in power. During his teens, Ivan began actively to intervene in the boyars' intrigues. By playing off one faction against the other, he gradually carved out an independent authority of his own. Eventually, in 1547, Ivan announced his own marriage and coronation as Tsar. On the eve of the celebrations, the young Prince ordered the execution of the factional leaders responsible for the mayhem of the previous years. The identity of his accomplices in this deed is not certain; but there were plenty of people in the capital who had experienced some past injustice at the hands of his victims.

3 The Reforms of the 1550s

The experiences of Ivan's minority had an important influence on the policy he adopted towards the boyars once he had come to power. By their actions during the 1530s and 1540s, the boyars had demonstrated to Ivan their strong disregard both for the welfare of the state and for the interests of the rightful ruler. Although it is improbable that Ivan ever intended the physical destruction of the boyar élite as a whole, he systematically endeavoured throughout his reign to reduce its influence and prestige.

It is a measure of Ivan's dissatisfaction with his boyars that he began to by-pass them in deciding matters of policy early on in his reign. During the 1550s, the new Tsar took advice from a 'Chosen Council', consisting largely of chancery officials and non-boyar favourites. On occasions, he threw open this circle and summoned various *pomeshchiki*, churchmen and merchants to participate in discussions.

The first years of Ivan's reign saw a flurry of reform. In the lawcode or *Sudebnik* which he promulgated in 1550, and in the church council, over which he presided the next year, Ivan paid special attention to the rooting out of corruption both in the state administration and in the ecclesiastical hierarchy. During this same period, he completed the work of bureaucratic reform begun by Ivan III and set up the last of the great chanceries which were to administer Muscovy until the eighteenth century: the department of foreign affairs; the *Razriad*; and the *pomeste-prikaz*.

These reforms were accompanied by determined efforts to rebuild and strengthen the class of *pomeshchiki* warriors. The *Razriad* and *pomeste-prikaz* were thus entrusted with the task of recovering *pomeste*-land taken by the boyars during Ivan's minority. At the same time, a series of decrees clarified the obligation of the peasantry to tend the estates of *pomeshchiki*-landowners.

The rise of the *pomeshchiki* to new influence and importance during Ivan's reign is exemplified in two actions undertaken during the 1550s.

In the first place, Ivan distributed a large part of his private domain in the Moscow region to about a 1000 *pomeshchiki*. On account of their proximity to the capital, the new tenants were able to act as Ivan's personal bodyguard and as a military reserve in times of crisis. Secondly, in 1555 Ivan abolished the institution of boyar provincial governors, replacing it with regional councils of *pomeshchiki*. By these measures, he took local affairs out of the hands of the boyar élite, while simultaneously providing himself with ready *pomeshchiki* support in the event of boyar resistance to his rule.

4 Ivan IV: An Exercise in Interpretation

Ever since the early nineteenth century, historians have commonly divided Ivan's reign into two halves. The first period coincides roughly with the institutional reforms of the 1550s, during which time Ivan is considered to have ruled wisely and moderately. The second period extends from about 1560 to his death in 1584. In this part of his reign Ivan is usually held to have behaved with pitiless cruelty and to have undertaken several irrational and bizarre experiments in government. The contrast between these two periods is so apparently marked that historians have frequently sought to explain the change in Ivan's conduct by reference to a deterioration in his mental condition. The usual explanation is that Ivan was driven insane either by the death of his first wife, Anastasia Romanov, in 1560, or as a consequence of having developed a disease of the spinal column which was so painful that it drove him frantic. An examination of Ivan's remains undertaken earlier this century yielded proof of skeletal deformity and thus the second explanation is usually considered the more likely.

Evidence for Ivan's exceptional savagery and irrationality rests on four main points, each of which is discussed in the extracts which follow. The first of these is the wholesale murder in which he apparently delighted, and which is demonstrated in particular by his violent persecution of the boyars (Source A) and of the inhabitants of Novgorod (Source B). The second is the decision he took in 1575 to install a temporary new Tsar on the curious grounds that it would teach his subjects a lesson (Source C). The third is the institution of the *opprichnina* whereby Ivan gave over a large portion of Muscovy to the sinister and murderous band of followers known as the *opprichniki* or 'children of darkness' (Source D). The fourth is the opinion given in the majority of sources, of which Source E is representative, that Ivan was unspeakably savage and brutal in his personal conduct.

Source A
The evidence of Sir Jerome Horsey, who met Ivan on several occasions and spent many years in Muscovy:

1 The Emperor's delight [was] making his chief exercise to devise
   and put in execution new torments, tortures and deaths, upon
   such as he took displeasure against and had in most jealousy,
   those especially of his nobility [boyars] of best credit and most
5 beloved of his subjects . . .

Source B
The evidence of a chronicler from the city of Novgorod, writing of
events which took place there in 1570:

1 The Tsar commanded that the powerful boyars, the important
   merchants, the administrative officials, and the citizens of every
   rank be brought before him, together with their wives and
   children. The Tsar ordered that they be tortured in his presence
5 in various spiteful, horrible and inhuman ways . . . their bodies
   tormented and roasted with fire in refined ways . . . and then
   thrown into the Volkhov River . . . Everyday perhaps a thousand
   human beings of all ages were thrown into the water and
   drowned . . .

Source C
Ivan explains to Daniel Sylvester, interpreter to the Muscovy Company, his motives for appointing a new Tsar:

1 The occasion [of this appointment] is the perverse and evil
   dealing of our subjects who murmur and repine at us; forgetting
   loyal obedience they practise against our person. The which to
   prevent we have given them over unto another prince to govern
5 them . . .

Source D
In a biography of Ivan IV, commonly attributed to the contemporary
Andrey Kurbsky, the following account is given of the 'children of
darkness' to whom Ivan entrusted control in a large portion of
Muscovy:

1 Instead of distinguished men adorned with good conscience, he
   gathered around him from all the land of Russia foul men, filled
   with every kind of evil, and furthermore, he bound them with
   terrible oaths and forced the accursed ones to have no dealings not
5 only with their friends and brethren, but also with their parents,
   and to please him in everything and to carry out his foul
   bloodthirsty orders. And on such terms, and on terms still fiercer
   than these, he forced the accursed and insane men to kiss the
   Cross . . . The Devil and his accomplice have armed the hosts of
10 the children of darkness . . . and bound them with vows and

Ivan IV: A Soviet representation from the 1930s

spells. [The author then proceeds to list all those boyars viciously slain by the 'children of darkness'.]

Source E
Giles Fletcher, who visited Muscovy as the ambassador of Queen Elizabeth of England, composed the following illustration of Ivan's conduct:

1 In his walks and progresses, if he had misliked the face or person of any man whom he met by the way, or that looked upon him, would command his head to be struck off. Which was presently done, and the head cast before him.

On the basis of descriptions such as those given above, historians have frequently asserted that Ivan suffered from strong delusions of persecution which gave rise to frequent acts of sadism. A number of other sources additionally suggest a strong element of sexual deviancy in Ivan's conduct.

For roughly a century now, a body of historians have argued that, despite the excesses of his reign, Ivan nevertheless pursued rational goals. Some have even argued that he was completely sane and suffered from no trace of mental illness. In proposing this point of view, 'revisionist' historians plainly contradict much of the evidence given in the sources. Their arguments for discarding this material are, however, cogent and they illuminate several important difficulties attending the analysis of Ivan's reign.

The literary evidence relating to the reign of Ivan IV is extraordinarily and demonstrably unreliable. Firstly, as Edward Keenan has argued (see 'Sources' on page 124), the writings attributed to Andrey Kurbsky, which make up the bulk of the surviving Muscovite evidence, consist of forgeries drawn up in the seventeenth century. The purpose behind this work of falsification is uncertain. Clearly, however, the Kurbsky documents on which historians of Ivan's reign have commonly relied, are of such doubtful origin that they no longer qualify as a useful source. Secondly, many of the other Muscovite accounts were composed after Ivan's death by the descendants or supporters of those boyar families which Ivan had excluded from influence. They are, therefore, highly partisan in their treatment of Ivan. Thirdly, the evidence of western visitors to Muscovy is equally suspect. Fletcher and Horsey, for instance, regularly confused fact with rumour and much of the detail they give has been exposed as false.

Revisionist historians of Ivan's reign do not go so far as to present the Tsar as a meek and moderate ruler, completely maligned by the surviving sources. Nor do they deny his responsibility for acts of brutality. Instead, they argue that Ivan had good grounds for suspecting some of his subjects of disloyalty and that, in the context of the sixteenth century, it was not unreasonable for Ivan to mete out harsh exemplary punishments.

As the Livonian War ground to a stalemate in the 1560s, Ivan became increasingly vulnerable to criticism. To begin with Ivan attempted to deflect resentment at Muscovy's military setbacks on to his Chosen Council, which he abolished on the grounds that it had advised him badly. The fall of the Chosen Council aroused the hopes of the boyars who saw an opportunity for recovering their influence. In time, individual boyars began to conspire to overthrow Ivan with the help of the Lithuanians. The leading citizens of Novgorod, who were anxious to regain their city's independence, were also implicated in various plots against Ivan.

Under these circumstances, so revisionist historians argue, it was entirely appropriate for Ivan to purge the ranks of his disloyal subjects and to seek to make a spectacular example of them. The political ideology of sixteenth-century Muscovy emphasised the importance of exemplary justice and extolled the merits of fierce reprisal actions. Faced, thus, with a challenge to his government, Ivan responded in the typical fashion of the strong Muscovite ruler. He lashed out in all directions, wreaking havoc in Novgorod, and decimating the ranks of the boyars in the four great purges of 1565, 1568, 1570 and 1575.

Hard evidence for this argument is lacking, and in particular we have no way of judging the extent and the seriousness of the plots made on Ivan's life. Nevertheless, some support for the revisionist interpretation may be found in the following account given by an English visitor to Muscovy.

Source F
Jerome Horsey describes the threats posed to Ivan's life and gives an illustration of his wish to make an example of traitors:

 1 The Emperor lived in great danger and fear of treasons and his
   making away, which he daily discovered; and spent much time in
   the examination, torturing, execution and putting to death [of]
   such noble captains and officers that were found practisers against
 5 him . . . Prince Boris Tulupov, discovered to be a treason worker
   against the Emperor, and confederate with the discontented
   nobility, was drawn upon a long, sharp-made stake, soaped to
   enter his fundament through his body which came out at his
   neck; upon which he languished for 15 hours . . . His mother
10 [there then follows an unrepeatable description which concludes
   with this 'goodly, matronly woman' being fed to dogs] . . . the
   Emperor at this sight saying, 'Such as I favour, I have honoured;
   and such as be traitors will I have thus done unto'.

In their analysis of Ivan's reigns, revisionist historians commonly

Issues Summary

Havering 6th Form College

23/06/2015

1

disregard the grim details of his career and look instead for evidence of intelligent and rational motives. In considering the above passage they would, therefore, ignore the grisly description of impalement and concentrate on the references to conspiracies and on Ivan's claim that he wished to make an example of traitors. In this way, Ivan's actions are made to seem rational and politically justified.

Let us now turn our attention from plots and punishments to some of the other curious features of Ivan's reign: his persecution of the boyars, his institution of the *opprichnina*, and his appointment of a Tsar to replace him. Let us see if in the account which follows we can discern a rational purpose for Ivan's actions.

Source G
The evidence of the Elizabethan envoy, Giles Fletcher:

1 Being a man of high spirit, and subtle in his mind, meaning to
  reduce his government into a more strict form, Ivan began by
  degrees to clip off the boyars' greatness, and to bring it down to a
  lesser proportion . . . so that now they hold their authorities,
5 lands, lives and all at the Emperor's pleasure, as the rest do. The
  means and practice whereby he wrought this to effect against
  those and other of the nobility were these . . .
  He divided his subjects into two parts or factions by a general
  schism. The one part he called the *opprichniki* or select men.
10 These were such of the nobility and gentry as he took to his own
  part, to protect and maintain them as his faithful subjects. The
  other he called *zemskii* or commons, which contained the base and
  vulgar sort, with such noblemen and gentlemen as he meant to
  cut off, as suspected to mislike his government . . .
15 The whole number of both parts was orderly registered and kept
  in a book: so that every man knew who was a *zemskii* man and
  who of the *opprichniki*. And the *opprichniki* had the liberty to spoil
  and kill the other, without any help of magistrate or law . . .
  Having thus pulled [the boyars], and ceased all their inheritance,
20 lands, privileges etc., save some very small part which he left to
  their name, he gave them other lands of the tenure of *pomeste* (as
  they call it), that are held at the Emperor's pleasure . . .
  Ivan used a very strange practice, that few princes would have
  done in their greatest extremities. He resigned his kingdom to one
25 Velica Knez Simeon . . . as though he meant to draw himself from
  all public doings to a quiet private life. Towards the end of the
  year, he caused the new King to call in all charters granted to
  bishoprics and monasteries, which they had enjoyed many hundred years before. Which were all cancelled. This done, he
30 resumed his sceptre and was content that they should renew their
  charters, reserving and annexing to the crown so much of their
  lands as himself thought good . .

If we examine Fletcher's account, we notice that Ivan's actions all seem to have a consistent purpose behind them: namely, the enrichment of the treasury and, in particular, the extension of the Tsar's private domain lands. The *opprichnina* thus appears as the instrument by which Ivan seized the lands of the boyars; the installation of the new Tsar seems a way of expropriating church properties. This brings us to the heart of the revisionist analysis of Ivan's reign: the desperate need for land which inspired and drove his domestic policies.

5   The Pokrovsky Model

The following section is the essential revisionist interpretation of Ivan's reign; it derives largely from the analysis put forward by the distinguished Russian and Soviet historian, N. M. Pokrovsky (1868–1932).

Throughout the second period of his reign, Ivan was engaged in a prolonged struggle with the Lithuanians and Swedes over the possession of Livonia (1558–82). The bulk of Muscovite armies committed to the Livonian War consisted of *pomeshchiki* warriors, who provided military support in return for land. In order to increase the number of *pomeshchiki* and thus the size of the army, Ivan needed to obtain more land to convert into *pomeste*-tenures. Crucially, however, by the second half of the sixteenth century, there was no further land readily available for this purpose. By the 1560s, most of the Tsar's private domain land had already been distributed; so had most of the common or 'black' land tilled by the peasantry. All that remained were church properties and the freehold estates or *votchina* of the boyars and large landowners. The ruler had no legal right to either type of property. They were not his to give away but were owned outright by their lords.

In order to obtain the land needed for his warriors Ivan was forced to resort to a number of illegal measures. In 1551 he attempted to secularise the extensive properties belonging to the church, but encountered such fierce clerical resistance that he was obliged to back down. He tried again in the 1570s, this time with apparently rather more success, using the ruse of a puppet-Tsar as a way of expropriating church lands.

The extensive *votchina*, owned by the boyars, were Ivan's chief target. Already in the 'decree on service' which he promulgated in 1556, Ivan had begun to undermine the concept of freehold property by instrucing the boyars to furnish set quantities of warriors from their *votchina* lands. In the 1560s, Ivan redoubled his efforts to reduce the *votchina* and to have them replaced with warrior-bearing *pomeste* tenures. For this purpose, he designated a large portion of Muscovy as *opprichnina* land and embarked on a ruthless programme of confiscation.

It is highly significant that the area of the *opprichnina* over which Ivan exercised control through the band of *opprichniki*, coincided closely with the territories wherein the largest share of *votchina* properties was concentrated. Indeed, the boundaries of the *opprichnina* were deliberately arranged in an irregular pattern, all the better to enclose boyar freehold land. No sooner had Ivan set up the *opprichnina* than he began seizing most of the *votchina* land which lay within its confines. He gave over this land to *pomeshchiki* straight away. In the execution of this task, the 'children of darkness' acted as the instruments of enforcement and eviction; hence their grim reputation. Over the course of the 1560s, Ivan added new swathes of territory to the *opprichnina*. Towns and marketplaces, even individual streets in Moscow, were all designated *opprichnina* property and redistributed by the Tsar. Thus, by the time the *opprichnina* was abolished in 1572, freehold property had ceased to play a significant role in Muscovy society.

Ivan's work of territorial reorganization was accomplished violently but without deliberate wholesale destruction. As Pokrovsky has pointed out, many of the old boyar families continued to hold influence at court throughout Ivan's reign. Ivan had no interest in exterminating the boyar élite and did not do so. Only those implicated in conspiracies against him were put to death. Unsurprisingly, though, as Ivan confiscated the boyars' property, an increasingly larger number of them actively engaged in plotting against him. Fierce reprisal actions were needed to put an end to this resistance.

According to Pokrovsky and the revisionist school of historians, Ivan's reign must be seen as the climax of the social revolution set in train by Ivan III a hundred years before. In the late fifteenth century, the first attempts had been made to create a new class of warrior-landowners on which the Grand Princes could rely for military and political support. Ivan completed the task of reform, converting the vast bulk of *votchina* properties into *pomeste* tenures, and elevating the *pomeshchiki* at the expense of the boyars. In this work of reconstruction, the institution of the *opprichnina* represented, in Pokrovsky's words, 'only the culminating point of a long socio-political process, which had begun long before Ivan, and which by its inexorable, elemental nature makes cogitation over "character" and "mental states" peculiarly idle'.

Many historians reject the Pokrovsky model as far too ambitious and as too insufficiently rooted in the sources. There is justice in this criticism; but the same charges may also be levelled at most other interpretations of Ivan's reign. If we argue that Ivan was driven by insanity, then we have to discount all evidence pointing to an underlying rationality of purpose. If we accept the reverse, that he was entirely sane, then we must explain the appalling reputation for brutality he enjoyed even within his own lifetime. Given the limitations of the surviving sources, a convincing case cannot be built for either interpretation. In the end, it will probably have to be accepted that there is just not enough firm evidence to remove once and for all the uncertainties attending Ivan's rule.

The title by which Ivan is known to posterity is similarly ambiguous. Within a short time of his death, Ivan had acquired the nickname of *Groznyi*. This may be variously translated as 'Terrible' or 'Majestic', for both elements are contained in the original Russian. 'Ivan the Terrible' or 'Ivan the Majestic'? Like so much else in Ivan's reign, it would seem that even Ivan's nickname is capable of more than one interpretation.

6 The Polish *Szlachta*

A comparative study of Muscovite and Polish political organization in the early modern period is a lesson in contrasts. In Muscovy, all authority was concentrated in the hands of the ruler, who held an absolute power unrestrained by any representative institutions. In the Polish–Lithuanian Commonwealth the power of the crown was limited, and the constitution provided for a division of authority between the King and the parliament or *Seym*. All laws required the consent of the *Seym*, in both its upper house or Senate, and in the elected Chamber of Deputies. Additionally, after 1573 the Polish and Lithuanian nobility, or *szlachta*, possessed the right of election to the crown and could thus choose whom it wanted as ruler.

For most of the early modern period, the Polish Commonwealth exhibited the principal characteristics of a 'mixed constitution' wherein power was shared and balanced between the ruler and his noble subjects. As the political theorist, Szymon Starowolski, explained in his *Polonia* (1632):

1 And so we have a King, not born to the throne but installed through election, who is the supreme executor of the laws passed by the *Seym*. We have a Senate, chosen from among the most notable gentry and appointed to look after the observance of these
5 laws. We have *Seym* deputies elected in a free vote [of the nobility] in each province, whose duty is to pass laws in parliament ... and who curb the King's power and the Senate's excessive authority.

★ The Polish nobles were extremely numerous. By the middle years of the sixteenth century, they accounted for about six per cent of the total population – some 500 000 out of 7.5 million. This proportion increased over the succeeding years, reaching about 10 per cent in the eighteenth century. Although the nobility constituted a single estate or *stan*, considerable differences persisted within its ranks. At the top of the noble hierarchy were the great magnates, who owned vast spreads of *latifundia*, particularly in the eastern, Lithuanian part of the Commonwealth. Many of these occupied the most important offices of state and they dominated the Senate. Below the magnates came the 'middling' gentry, made up of the smaller noble landowners. The vast majority of Polish nobles were however landless. Although the 'noble-men in clogs' formed the backbone of their estate, their material condition was almost indistinguishable from that of serfs. Often landless gentry hired themselves out as rural labourers; alternatively they sought employment in the households of the magnates. All, however, proudly displayed their ancient armorial bearings, swaggered down the muddy lanes with their wooden swords (steel ones being too expensive), and dutifully gathered together every few years at their local parliaments or *seymiki*. At these events, the nobles elected representatives to attend the Chamber of Deputies in the *Seym*.

Originally, the Polish noblemen were distinguished by the military obligation which they owed the King. During the later middle ages, the nobles had gradually extended their political power at the expense of the crown. Following the extinction of the Piast dynasty in 1370, the nobles were regularly able to extract concessions from the ruler in return for giving him their support against potential rivals and for guaranteeing the succession in his family. In the earliest example of this exchange, King Louis in 1374 had exempted the Polish nobles from payment of all taxes in return for the recognition of his daughter's right of inheritance. King Jogaila and his descendants, in order to keep the crown in their family, had similarly been obliged to extend the privileges of the nobility. Freedom from arbitrary arrest and the right to be consulted in all important matters of state were the principal concessions extracted by the Polish gentry from the crown. By the terms of the Union of Lublin (1569) all these rights were automatically acquired by the Lithuanian nobility.

* Despite the growing power of the nobles, the authority remaining to the King was still substantial. As an Irish visitor to Poland later remarked:

1 He [the King] has the free nomination of all ecclesiastical benefices, and of all secular employments, as well military and civil throughout the whole extent of his dominions; without speaking of a great number of royal demesnes, which together
5 with state dignities he confers on those that have deserved them. He can bestow as considerable preferments as any prince in Europe, and oblige and raise the fortunes of whom he pleases . . . He can call, prorogue and dissolve the diet [*Seym*] at pleasure. In a word, the Poles term him, the Protector of their laws and
10 privileges; the Distributor of honours; the Supreme head of their Republic [Commonwealth]; and Supreme General of their forces.

By judicious use of patronage, and by manipulating the meetings and agenda of the *Seym*, the Kings of Poland were able to preserve both their authority and the balance of power between crown and *szlachta*.

Throughout the sixteenth century, the Kings of Poland calculated that the magnates who dominated the Senate constituted the foremost challenge to the crown. By virtue of their huge landed wealth and their private armies of retainers, many of the magnates possessed an influence which allowed them to defy the King with impunity. Accordingly, the Kings of Poland adopted the policy of co-operating with the leaders of the gentry, who for their part were wary of the magnates' power in the regions. In 1505, in the statute *Nihil Novi*, the King granted to the Chamber of Deputies, the organ of the poorer gentry, the same rights as he had previously been obliged to grant the Senate. Hereafter, the *Seym* deputies might in a collective vote defeat any innovation of law or government to which they were opposed. In a similar bid to outmanoeuvre the magnates, the Polish Kings continually recruited members of the gentry into the royal administration. Employed either as secretaries in the chancellery or as local sheriffs, noblemen of humble origin acted as an important counterweight to the influential magnates who dominated the Senate and large tracts of the countryside. Here, there is an obvious parallel with the policies pursued by both Ivan III of Muscovy and his descendants.

    * During the course of the sixteenth century, leading members of the Polish gentry gradually acquired a sense of their political importance and developed a programme of their own. The 'Executionists', those noblemen committed to the proper execution or enforcement of the country's laws, championed a series of reforms which had the double effect of limiting the influence of the magnates while simultaneously advancing the power of the crown. During the 1560s, a large number of royal estates previously alienated to the magnates were repossessed by the King at the instigation of Executionist deputies. Over the same period, the number of crown offices which an individual magnate might hold was similarly cut back by instruction of the *Seym*. The reorganization of the judicial administration and of the treasury, again undertaken at the behest of the Chamber of Deputies, added to the influence of the monarchy and suggested the overall success of its partnership with the gentry.

    The Executionist party was, however, determined to consolidate its influence over both magnates and sovereign. In 1572, King Sigismund II died. Although the crown was in theory elective, up to this point only the more prominent noblemen, meeting in a throng at court, had played a part in the selection process. Invariably, they had chosen a close relative of the dead King as their new lord. Sigismund was, however, without family and had no obvious successor. In the absence of a natural heir, the leading Executionists seized the initiative. At a gathering of the *Seym* at Warsaw in 1573, they forced through the principle that all noblemen in the Commonwealth had the right to direct participation in the King's election. Next, they bartered with the various aspirants for the throne (there were five altogether) and adopted the cause of the candidate who promised the most. He, as it turned out, was the French prince, Henry of Anjou. In return for his tumultuous election, roared out by some 40000 noblemen on a field outside the capital, Henry agreed to a series of measures which put the partnership of crown and *Seym* on a firm constitutional footing. The 'Henrician Articles' laid down that the *Seym* was henceforward to meet every two years, and that the King could neither raise taxes, nor go to war, nor marry without the *Seym's* consent. Any failure on the King's part to honour these obligations made him liable to deposition. After Henry, all the Kings of Poland had in return for election to agree to the Henrician Articles and to any other articles which the *Seym* saw fit to impose. These preconditions or *Pacta Conventa* severely hampered the crown's capability of independent action.

* During the last decades of the sixteenth century, the deputies of the *Seym* gradually began to accept the principle that their decisions needed the unanimous approval of all the deputies in order to be valid. The objection or *liberum veto* of a single noble deputy could thus defeat any proposal submitted in the *Seym* even if it had the support of the majority. To begin with, the right of *liberum veto* was used sparingly. It was only towards the end of the seventeenth century that the passage of legislation was seriously disrupted by misuse of the *veto*. Nevertheless, the development of this unusual constitutional device indicates the nobility's attachment to the idea that individual rights should never be jeopardised by 'the tyranny of the majority'. The much vaunted 'Golden Liberty' of the Polish–Lithuanian *szlachta* involved, above all, the freedom of its members to obstruct all such proposals as threatened individual interests.

* Uniquely in contemporary Europe, Poland was spared conflict over religion. Reformation ideas certainly took root in the country. Lutheranism was prevalent in the cities, and many of the nobility embraced Calvinism. A medley of smaller Protestant sects, Anabaptists, Mennonites, Arians and Unitarians, also established themselves in the kingdom which already had substantial pockets of Armenian, Orthodox and Jewish believers. Nevertheless, even after the onset of the Counter-Reformation, persecution and violence never afflicted relations between the various faiths. In the Confederation of Warsaw, drawn up by the *Seym* in 1573, the principle of toleration and peaceful coexistence was written into the country's laws:

1 Whereas in our commonwealth there is no small disagreement in the matter of the Christian faith, and in order to prevent that any harmful contention should arise from this, as we see clearly taking place in other kingdoms, we swear to each other in our name and
5 in that of our descendants for ever more . . . that albeit we are *dissidentes in religione*, we will keep the peace between ourselves and we will not for the sake of various faiths and differences of churches, either shed blood or confiscate property, deny favour,

The Royal Election of 1764 by Bernardo Bellotto. The throne stands empty in the middle of the enclosure. Outside the enclosure are voters, the szlachta, fully armed on horseback and drawn up in military order.

imprison or banish, and that furthermore we will not aid or abet
10 any power or office which strives to this in any way whatsoever . . .

This law applied not only to the nobility but to the peasantry and
townsfolk as well, and almost certainly accounts for the harmonious
relations between the churches in Poland. (The Protestant martyrology
for Poland manages in the century after 1550 a mere dozen persons.) In
this way, the Golden Liberty of the Polish *szlachta* amounted to rather
more than the liberty of the nobles to participate fully in the political
life of the Commonwealth. The emphasis on individual rights and
freedoms championed by the *Seym* gave all the King's subjects a liberty
of conscience and worship quite unprecedented in European history.

Making notes on 'Government and Politics'

This chapter is primarily concerned with internal developments in
Muscovy and in Poland during the sixteenth century. The sections
devoted to Ivan IV occupy about a half of the chapter and introduce a
number of important problems of historical interpretation. They do
not, however, provide answers to whether Ivan was mad or sane or to
whether he pursued rational or irrational policies. What they try and do
is to lead you to a consideration of the problems attending Ivan's reign
by analysing some of the sources for the period. The following
headings, questions and tasks should help you to make notes:
1.   Chanceries and *pomeshchiki*
1.1. The development of the chanceries
1.2. Secretaries and boyars
1.3. The *pomeshchiki*. Feudalism has been defined by one historian of
political institutions as a system involving, 'a social hierarchy
based on the tenure of land, jurisdiction by landlords over their
tenants, and the granting of land in return for service, particularly
military services, to the King or lord from whom the land was
held.' By this measure, did the establishment of the *pomeshchiki*
amount to the introduction of feudalism to Muscovy?
2.   The boyars and the minority of Ivan IV
2.1. The boyars before Ivan IV's accession
2.2. Boyar misrule

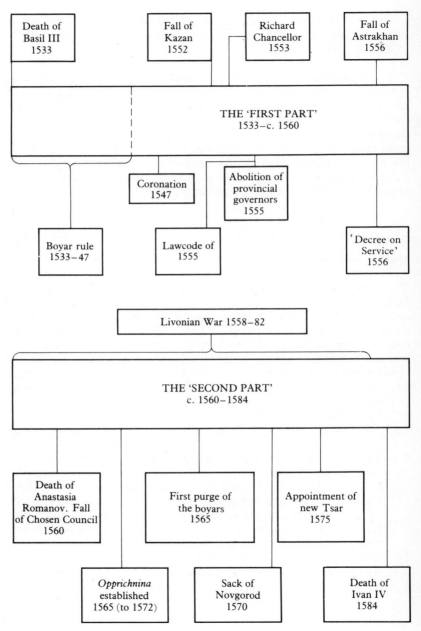

The reign of Ivan IV

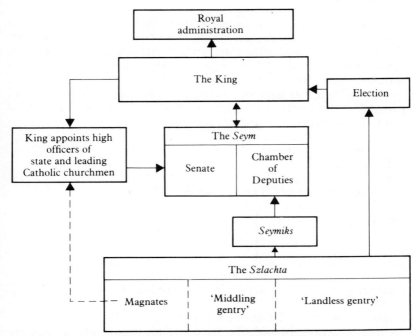

The organization of the Polish–Lithuanian Commonwealth, c. 1590

3. The reforms of the 1550s. To what extent did Ivan IV build on and continue the work of his predecessors?
4. Ivan IV: An Exercise in Interpretation
5. The Pokrovsky Model

Note these last two sections together by reference to the exercise given below. Make sure before you start writing that you follow the broad outline of the various arguments you encounter in these sections. Since they approach Ivan's reign analytically rather than chronologically, you may wish to refer to the date-chart given on page 58. Divide a sheet of paper into five columns:

Source	Brief outline of contents	Reliability of source	Evidence of insanity	Evidence of rational purpose

Under 'Source' jot down the name of the author of each of the passages A–G; then, in the next column give a brief summary of the contents of each passage; next, assess the reliability of the source by reference to what you know or may presume about its author; after this, write down the evidence contained in the extract which suggests that Ivan was mad; finally (and this will need to be your widest column) explain how a revisionist historian might go about justifying or explaining Ivan's conduct. When you have completed this exercise, outline in a brief paragraph either your own opinion of Ivan's rule or the reasons why you feel it appropriate to reserve judgement.

6.   The Polish *szlachta*
6.1. A mixed constitution
6.2. The nobility
6.3. Royal resources
6.4. The Executionists. The election of 1573
6.5. The *liberum veto*
6.6. Religion

Answering essay questions on 'Government and Politics'

A-level questions on the domestic policies of Ivan IV are frequent and are usually concerned with the impact of his personality or with the tensions to which his reign gave rise:

1. '"Its meaning is best sought in the realms of psychology". Discuss this verdict on the reign of Ivan IV of Muscovy.'

2. 'How disastrous for Muscovy was the reign of Ivan IV?'

In tackling this type of question, you should neither give a chronological outline of Ivan's reign nor confine your account to a single interpretation of his career. The chances are that if you write a straightforward biographical answer you will include much material not of direct relevance and fail therefore to tackle the question directly. If you adopt a revisionist or traditionalist interpretation alone, you will omit fruitful lines of enquiry and give your essay too narrow a focus.

Many A-level questions can be usefully answered in the form of 'thesis, antithesis, synthesis'. This method allows you to give the subject of the question a full consideration while at the same time imposing a rigorous structure on your argument. Firstly, marshall all the evidence and information known to you in the form of one point of view (the thesis); then, gather all the material which might be used to favour the opposite case (the antithesis). The synthesis should be your concluding attempt to steer a midway course between the two opposite opinions and to arrive at a balanced judgement. What evidence would you put forward in favour of the opinion that the meaning of Ivan's reign is best sought 'in the realms of psychology' or that his rule was damaging to Muscovy? What evidence is there to support an opposite point of view? What is your own balanced opinion about his reign?

There have been A-level questions on sixteenth-century Poland. Rarely, admittedly, but when they have occurred they have been absolutely straightforward:

3. 'What were the principal features of the political organization of sixteenth-century Poland?'

Section 6 of this chapter is deliberately geared towards the answering of just such a question. However, in composing your answer, you should endeavour to make your own mark on the material. What in your opinion were the most important and exceptional aspects of political organization in the Commonwealth? What was unusual about it? The power of the nobility? The role of the parliament? Electoral kingship? Responses such as these will provide you with a framework around which you can build your answer.

Source-based questions on 'Government and Politics'

1 Ivan IV
Read sources A–G on pages 44 to 50, and look at the picture of Ivan IV on page 46 taken from Eisenstein film, *Ivan the Terrible*. Answer the following questions:
a) How do these sources portray Ivan IV's character and personality? To what extent is the opinion presented in the sources shared by the twentieth-century depiction of Ivan IV?
b) How reliable as evidence do you judge the body of writings attributed to Andrey Kurbsky and the accounts given by contemporary English travellers to Muscovy?
c) Using the evidence contained in Source F, explain how Ivan's savage treatment of Novgorod (Source B) might have been justified at the time?
d) Using the information given in Source G, and any other information known to you, explain the extent to which Ivan's political actions may have been determined by the need to obtain fresh land for his warriors?

2 The Polish *Szlachta*
Read the extract taken from Starowolski's *Polonia* on page 52, the account of the Irish visitor on page 53, and the extract taken from

the 1573 Confederation of Warsaw on page 55. Answer the following questions:

a) What do you understand by the term 'mixed constitution'? What evidence is contained in the first extract to suggest that the Commonwealth had a political organization which fits into this category?

b) Explain in your own words the powers belonging to the King, as outlined by the Irish visitor. How might the sovereign use these powers so as to tip the political balance in his favour?

c) For what reasons might it be said that developments in *Seym* procedure in the later sixteenth century made the practice of religious toleration inevitable in Poland?

CHAPTER 4

The Seventeenth Century

1 The Muscovite 'Time of Troubles'

a) Platonov's 'Three Phases'

The 'Time of Troubles' was a particularly violent and turbulent period of Muscovite history which extended from the extinction of the House of Rurik in 1598 to the establishment of the Romanov dynasty in 1613. This span of 15 years witnessed a succession of civil wars, foreign invasions and peasant uprisings. As the social and political structure established over the preceding century began to collapse, the very survival of the unitary Muscovite state was threatened. Only the timely election of Michael Romanov as Tsar halted the slide towards territorial fragmentation and partition.

Historians of the 'Time of Troubles' have frequently sought to divide the conflicts of this period into three separate phases: a 'dynastic phase'; a 'social phase'; and a phase of 'national struggle' against foreign intervention. According to this scheme, first proposed by S. F. Platonov in the 1920s, the death without heir of Tsar Fedor (Theodore) in 1598 led immediately to a violent struggle for the throne. In the turmoil which followed, pent-up social tensions were suddenly released, prompting widespread peasant revolts. Taking advantage of the mayhem, Swedish and Polish troops overran Muscovy, thereby adding to the chaos. Ultimately, however, this foreign intervention caused the warring parties in Russia to put aside their quarrels and to work together to restore order.

Although the 'three-phase' model of the 'Time of Troubles' doubt-less involves an oversimplification of events, analysis of the period 1598–1613 along the lines proposed by Platonov is still a useful way of illuminating the more important features of this confusing episode of Muscovite history.

b) The 'Dynastic Phase'

The cause of the 'Time of Troubles' may be traced back to the death of Ivan IV. Ivan's heir was his son Fedor, who inherited the throne in 1584. Fedor was renowned for his piety, for his love of bell-ringing, and for his extreme reluctance to become involved in affairs of state. Under these circumstances, it was inevitable that others would rule in his name. Almost at once, the leading role in government was assumed by

Fedor's brother-in-law, Boris Godunov, who had risen to prominence at court during the reign of Ivan IV.

Of Fedor's two brothers, the first had perished in 1582 (slain according to some accounts by Ivan IV personally) and the second, Dmitri, had died 10 years later as a consequence of an epileptic fit. Fedor was left, therefore, the last surviving male representative of the House of Rurik, the princely dynasty which could trace its descent back to the Varangian rulers of medieval Kiev. Nevertheless, despite his marriage and much urging to sire a son, Fedor remained heirless. His death in 1598 consequently plunged Muscovy into chaos. No procedure existed for selecting a successor in the unprecedented circumstance of the ruler dying with neither heir nor close kin.

* In the months following Fedor's death, Godunov conducted a vigorous campaign aimed at winning the throne for himself. To this end, he enlisted the support of leading churchmen and of a large section of the *pomeshchiki*. Nevertheless, for all the acclamations attending Boris's eventual coronation in September 1598, his kingship rested on insecure foundations. Since Boris was not of the House of Rurik, he was widely considered to be a usurper. Thus from the very first, he encountered powerful opposition both from those boyars who felt he had no greater right to rule than they, and from simple folk who saw no reason to obey a Prince not descended from the ancient family of Tsars.

During Boris's reign, the phenomenon of pretendership made its first appearance in Russia. Rival candidates for the throne appeared who announced themselves to be long-lost scions of the House of Rurik. Altogether in the period 1598–1613, some 40 such pretenders staked a claim to the crown and led rebellions against the ruler in Moscow. Since neither Boris nor his immediate successors enjoyed a firm right to the throne, pretendership often became a way of expressing dissatisfaction with the regime in power.

* The earliest of the pretenders was Grishka Otrepev, a defrocked monk who had spent some time in Poland. In 1603 he announced himself to be Dmitri, Fedor's half-brother, long believed dead. Otrepev's claim was patently absurd. Nevertheless, his cause received support both from Tsar Boris's boyar rivals and from several Polish–Lithuanian magnates who had previously made Otrepev's acquaintance and who now sought to profit territorially from the deception. Although Otrepev managed to rally considerable support for his cause, it was only after the death of Godunov in 1605 that the 'False Dmitri' was able to obtain his coronation as Tsar.

Otrepev was both an intelligent and an unusual ruler. He was attentive to the business of government and to the needs of his subjects, and he embarked on an ambitious programme of domestic reform. Masquerade had, however, become such a way of life for him that he regularly employed a double to officiate at public gatherings and, on other occasions, appeared himself wearing a false beard. But it was not so much his duplicity as his evidently pro-Polish sympathies that brought about his downfall. With a Polish wife and entourage of Jesuit priests, Otrepev aroused deep distrust in Moscow. His claim to the throne was widely suspected of being fraudulent. Additionally, his religious preferences appeared Catholic rather than orthodox. Within a few months Otrepev was overthrown and slain by a rioting mob in the capital. According to legend, this man of disguises continued for some time to haunt the land in the shape of a werewolf.

It seems probable that the death of Otrepev was organized by a group of boyars led by Basil Shuisky, for no sooner was the 'False Dmitri' dead than Shuisky had seized the throne for himself. Once in power as Basil IV, Shuisky justified his usurpation on the grounds that he was himself distantly related to the House of Rurik, and that he enjoyed the full confidence of his subjects. As Basil pronounced in 1606:

1 We the Great Sovereign, Tsar and Grand Prince of All Russia, by
  the grace of God and by the entreaty of our pious metropolitans,
  archbishops, bishops, and the entire holy council, and by the
  petitions of the boyars, lessers boyars, nobles, and sundry men of
5 the Muscovite state, and by our own descent, have established
  ourselves in the Muscovite state as Sovereign, Tsar, and Grand
  Prince of All Russia; and with God's help we wish to maintain the
  Muscovite state as did our ancestors, the Great Sovereigns and
  Tsars of Russia . . .

For all these fine boasts, Basil's occupation of the throne met with widespread disapproval. According to one contemporary chronicle:

1 The aforementioned Basil, without the consent of the people of
  the entire land, by chance and hurriedly . . . was first acclaimed in
  his own courtyard and then installed as Tsar of All Great Russia,
  solely by the people who were present here in the ruling city . . .
5 He was able to act so shamelessly only because no one dared to
  oppose him or to contradict him in this great matter . . . Quickly
  without delay, and hastily without deliberation, he ascended to
  the highest place; unlike the usurpers who preceded him, he did
  not try to win the lesser people over to him. As a result he was
10 hated by the people . . . and it rose up against him in violent war.

c) The 'Social Phase'

Muscovite Russia was populated largely by peasants. In the main, the peasantry dwelled and worked in village communes under the leadership of elected headmen. This form of co-operative organization was made necessary by the foreshortened growing season which put a premium on collective effort and teamwork. During the middle ages, the majority of peasants worked on the common or 'black' land, which they cultivated and tilled as if it were indeed their own property. Legally, however, all 'black' land belonged to the Prince and in token of this the commune paid him a nominal rent.

The introduction of *pomeste*-landholding by Ivan III brought about a rapid deterioration in the peasants' lot. A large portion of the 'black' land was given away by the ruler to the new class of *pomeshchiki*. Along with the land went the peasants who worked it. In return for accompanying the Tsar on campaigns, the *pomeshchiki* were expected to make a living from the lands they had been given, as well as to furnish a horse, armour and retainers. In order to meet their military obligations, the *pomeshchiki* sought to extract more from their peasants. Rents were pushed up and the peasantry were made to devote an increasing share of their time to working on their masters' private estates.

At the same time, the power of the landowners over the local peasantry was augmented. Many of the functions hitherto performed by the commune were taken over by the *pomeshchiki*. They organized the collection of taxes, and regularly appointed stewards to take the place of elected headmen. By the middle years of the sixteenth century, it was normal for the local *pomeste* landholder to exercise full judicial and police powers over his peasants.

The response of the peasantry to these new impositions was obvious: they simply left their villages and flooded in great waves to those places where 'black' land was still available and where the system of *pomeste*-tenure had not yet been introduced. In the main, the peasants descended on the newly-won territories of the lower and middle Volga and eastwards in the direction of Siberia. The flight of the peasantry from the central portions of Muscovy to the periphery is well documented. When Richard Chancellor visited Moscow in the 1550s, he passed by lands 'very well replenished with small villages which are so well filled with people it is a wonder to see them'. Giles Fletcher made the same journey 30 years later and noticed how, 'many villages and towns of half a mile and a mile long stand all uninhabited, the people being fled all into other places by reason of the extreme usage and exactions done unto them'.

The flight of the peasantry threatened the entire system of *pomeste*-landholding and thus the basis of military provision in Muscovy. Accordingly, the Tsars took urgent action to halt the tide of depopulation. Starting in the 1490s, a series of restrictions began to be imposed on peasant movement. By 1600, the peasantry had all but lost the right to leave their place of residence. Tied thus to the soil, compelled to perform labour services for the local lords, and subordinated to the jurisdiction of the landowners' courts, the peasantry were steadily reduced to the condition of serfs.

The development of serfdom had an important effect on Muscovy's towns. These had always been small in comparison to their west European counterparts and few had contained a population of more than a few thousand. The reversion to a primitive manorial economy and the prohibition on movement hindered the establishment of an urban merchant class. The impoverished peasants had insufficient wealth to purchase commodities and, since they were tied to the land, the towns were deprived of the workforce needed to develop manufacturing and industrial enterprises. It was partly the continued underdevelopment of its towns which accounted for Muscovy's economic backwardness and retardation.

The process of feudalisation and enserfment was greatly resented by the peasants who had no wish to lose their personal, legal and economic freedoms. Under these circumstances, it is hardly surprising that the outbreak of civil war in Muscovy acted as a signal for peasant rebellion. During the reign of Basil IV, the brushfires of revolt which had been smouldering ever since the accession of Boris Godunov, burst into a mighty conflagration. Under the leadership of another 'Tsar Dmitri', a peasant army established itself just outside the capital. Manifestos published by the rebels called on serfs to murder their masters and to seize their wealth. For several years, the rabble troops of 'False Dmitri II' held much of the countryside in their thrall. Even after Dmitri's death in 1610, his son and successor continued to provide a rallying point for the disaffected and dispossessed.

d) The Phase of 'National Struggle'

The deep political and social crisis which afflicted Muscovy during the first years of the seventeenth century opened the way to foreign intervention. Already during the reign of False Dmitri I, individual Polish and Lithuanian lords had, with the ruler's connivance, helped themselves to parts of Russian territory. Dmitri–Otrepev's murder put only a temporary halt to their plundering. In order to establish a counterweight to the Polish lords and to gain help against the peasant army of False Dmitri II, Basil Shuisky sought the assistance of Charles IX of Sweden. Charles had designs on Muscovite territory and trade, and promptly used the invitation as an excuse to invade Muscovy.

The Swedish involvement drew in its turn a decisive response from the Polish Commonwealth. In 1609 Sigismund III of Poland invaded Muscovy and announced the candidature of his son for the Muscovite throne. As the Poles advanced on Moscow, capturing Smolensk on the way, the opposing army of Swedes put Novgorod under siege. Meanwhile, outside Moscow a peasant army ravaged the countryside. Inside the capital, a 'Council of Boyars' overthrew Basil Shuisky and vainly tried to preserve what little authority was left to the government.

* It was at this time of foreign invasion and domestic turmoil that a new force entered the confusion of Muscovite politics. During the

months following Basil IV's deposition, local militias were established in a number of centres and rapidly coalesced into a united organization. The avowed objective of the militia leaders was to rid the country of foreign invaders and to re-establish the monarchy on a firm and lasting basis. As one militia commander explained, 'If we have no sovereign, our realm completely falls apart'.

The inspiration behind the new organization appears to have been a combination of townsmen and clergy. However, the backbone of the militias consisted of *pomeshchiki*, gathered in the main from the regions around Smolensk and the upper Volga. Many of these had had their estates plundered or confiscated in the turmoil of the preceding years, and they were anxious for a return to orderly conditions. In recognition of the importance of the *pomeshchiki* to their cause, the militia leaders rapidly established their own 'service-tenure chancery'. The purpose of this institution was to draw up new land registers and to see to the proper apportionment of estates to dispossessed *pomeshchiki*.

Soviet historians are fond of portraying the militias as a 'national army', swept to success on a tide of popular patriotism. This may well be, although it is always hard to measure the impact on people of such sentiments as patriotism. The rapid success of the militias probably owed as much to the diplomatic and military skills of their commanders, to the support of the *pomeshchiki* and to the large amounts of wealth which found their way into militia coffers. By confiscating the property of their opponents and by imposing a heavy 'loyalty tax' on their supporters, the militia leaders acquired sufficient funds to fit out an army. With a mixed body consisting of about 10 000 *pomeshchiki* and local levies, the militia commander, Prince Pozharsky, defeated a numerically stronger force of Poles in August 1612. Shortly afterwards, he captured Moscow.

* There remained the problem of a Tsar. Past experience had shown how vital it was that any new ruler should enjoy wide popular confidence and not appear a usurper. The solution adopted by the militia leaders to the question of legitimacy was really no more than to extend the principle by which they themselves held power. The organization of the militias was essentially a democratic one based on the traditions of the old peasant commune. Elected councils administered the raising of taxes and troops, while supreme authority in army affairs was vested in the 'Steward and Commander Elected by the Whole People of the Muscovite Realm and All Ranks of People, Military and Civilian'.

In November 1612 the militia leaders summoned a 'council of the whole land' to meet in Moscow 'to elect a sovereign by the whole land, whomsoever the merciful God shall grant us'. Altogether some 700 people, mainly townsmen and *pomeshchiki*, attended the gathering. Surviving writs of summons suggest that a primitive form of popular election did indeed lie behind the choice of deputies.

According to the record of events, the gathering in Moscow was attended 'with much excitement, everyone wanting to act according to his own ideas, everyone advocating someone else'. The champion of the *pomeshchiki* and of the Moscow militia garrison was the young Michael Romanov, whose great aunt Anastasia Romanov had been the first wife of Ivan IV. Although the blood of the House of Rurik did not flow in Michael's veins, some of the charisma of the old Tsar attached to him. With the support of 'many *pomeshchiki*, lesser boyars, merchants from numerous towns and Cossacks', Michael was acclaimed the new Tsar in February 1613.

2 The Romanov Recovery

'Few examples can be found in history when a new sovereign ascended the throne in conditions so extremely sad as those in which Michael [Romanov] was elected.' With these words, a nineteenth-century Russian historian summarised the legacy of the 'Time of Troubles'. In the year of Michael's accession (1613), Polish and Swedish troops remained in occupation of large portions of Muscovy; bands of peasants still roamed the countryside; and the system of law and administration had all but ceased to function. Muscovy's recovery from these dismal conditions owed much to the cautious policies of Tsars Michael (1613–45) and Alexey (1645–76), and in particular to their close partnership with, and timely abandonment of, the *pomeshchiki*.

Tsar Michael pursued an unadventurous course in foreign affairs, avoiding conflict and making concessions as required. A necessary first step was to secure the removal of the Polish and Swedish armies which had established themselves on Muscovite soil over the previous decade. In 1617 he obtained the departure of the Swedes by handing over territories in Karelia to King Gustavus Adolphus. The next year he recognised the Polish conquest of Smolensk in return for the Commonwealth evacuating its forces from the rest of the country. Smolensk was a heavy loss, for it represented Muscovy's 'gateway to the west' and was also the site of her most formidable border fortress. Michael's failure to recapture the city in 1632 and the defeat he suffered on this occasion only confirmed his decision to avoid in future all such costly military engagements.

* Michael owed his election to the *pomeshchiki* warriors. They had made up the bulk both of the militia units which had captured Moscow, and of the assembly which had appointed him Tsar. Additionally, the *pomeshchiki* continued to provide the core of the Muscovite army and constituted the Tsar's principal defence against both foreign attack and internal rebellion.

Throughout his reign, Michael took care to reward and to nurture the *pomeshchiki*. As one of his earliest actions he ordered an investigation of the activities of the 'strong people' who had helped themselves

over the preceding years to much *pomeshchiki* property. Most importantly, a series of decrees promulgated in the 1620s and 1630s
established *pomeste*-holdings as hereditary, and limited the number of
pomeshchiki only to those who could claim descent from a *pomeshchik*
forebear. By these measures, Michael effectively converted the *pomeshchiki* into the privileged and hereditary class known to historians as the
dvoriane or 'service-nobility'.

   * The Romanov partnership with the service-nobility is exemplified
in the institution of the *Zemski Sobor* or 'National Assembly'. Michael
retained the assembly which had put him in power and throughout his
reign he frequently consulted with this body in matters of domestic and
foreign policy. Membership of the assembly was evidently determined
by some form of election, and service-noblemen attended its meetings
both regularly and in large numbers. It was the particular function of
the assemblies to draw up petitions for the Tsar's consideration and to
advise on how 'to carry out such reform in all matters as may be best for
the Muscovite state'. The institution of the *Zemski Sobor* achieved its
high point of influence in 1648 when it saw to the promulgation of the
lawcode or *Ulozhenie* which established on a lasting basis the special
rights and privileges of the Muscovite nobility.

   A number of historians have detected in the *Zemski Sobor* an
incipient parliament. This cannot be the case. Although a representative element was certainly involved in these gatherings, the assemblies
lacked most of the distinguishing features of representative institutions
elsewhere in Europe. They enjoyed no powers in the matter of
revenue-raising and thus had no pull on the Tsar's purse-strings. No
procedures were laid down as to how the assembly should conduct its
business and its rights in relation to the crown were never established.
The Tsar called and dismissed the assembly at will, and on several
important occasions he deliberately excluded it from any part in
decision-making.

   In essence, the *Zemski Sobor* was a 'child of chaos', born of the
confused circumstances which ended the 'Time of Troubles' and
succoured only because the Tsar still needed the support of the
pomeshchiki-dvoriane. Once it had become apparent that the monarchy
no longer depended for survival on the support of this group, the
assembly was allowed to wither. After 1653 it met no more.

   * Even during the first decades of Michael Romanov's reign, when
the partnership of Tsar and noblemen seemed at its height, the Tsar
was endeavouring to limit his dependence on the *dvoriane*. The central
administrative organs, the *prikazy* chanceries, continued therefore to be
staffed by officials drawn from the wealthier families living around
Moscow and were not opened up to the humbler nobles. Importantly
also, the councils which administered law and justice in the localities
and which were dominated by *dvoriane*, were steadily superseded.
Voevodas, or military governors, were appointed by the Tsar over the

provinces and given full responsibility for all policing and judicial functions. The institutions of noble supremacy in the countryside were thus squeezed out by agents of the central government.

During the reign of Alexey Romanov, the ascendancy of the *dvoriane* in the Muscovite military organization was broken. It had long been recognised that the *pomeshchiki* cavalry were ill prepared for the new types of warfare practised by Muscovy's European neighbours. The only tactic known to the cavalry was to charge *en masse* at the enemy in the hope of using their sabres and spears at close quarters. They were thus no match for the cannon, pikemen and musketeers deployed in increasing numbers by Muscovy's rivals. In order to make up for this deficiency, a corps of about 5000 regular musketeers or *streltsy* had been formed in the sixteenth century.

Under the Romanovs, the corps of *streltsy* was first enlarged and then in the 1640s superseded entirely by units of trained and drilled infantrymen. New regiments composed mainly of peasant conscripts and staffed by foreign officers were gradually introduced on a permanent, standing basis during Alexey's reign. By 1663 Muscovy had some 60 000 of these regular troops, all capable of discharging a firearm in battle, of advancing under an artillery barrage, and of undertaking long sieges. Although a number of the poorer *dvoriane* were drafted into these regiments of 'the new order', the nobles were for the most part confined to guard duties.

The cost of the new type of military provision was met by increased taxation and by the systematic debasement of the coinage. The hardships and inflation brought about by these methods of raising revenue were partly responsible for a new spate of peasant risings in the 1660s and 1670s.

The professionalisation of the army had the effect of robbing the *dvoriane* of their position of power in the Muscovite military organization. By the same token, the new regiments freed the Tsar from his reliance on the *dvoriane* at time of war or unrest. Having thus rebuilt the state and government in alliance with the *pomeshchiki*, the Romanov Tsars found themselves in the fortunate position of being able to dispense with their support. As a consequence, the withering of the *Zemski Sobor* and the abolition of the local councils was not attended by any challenge to the authority of the Tsar. In future, the Tsarist autocracy would rest its power on a subservient army and, under Peter the Great, would transform itself into a military despotism.

3 The Khmelnitzky Revolt

The 'Time of Troubles' and the first uneasy years of Romanov rule gave Poland a welcome opportunity in which to extend and consolidate her eastern frontiers. In 1611, the Poles seized Smolensk. Their occupation of this important city and fortress was recognised by Tsar Michael in

1619 and confirmed in 1634. Over the same period, the Polish settlement and conquest of the Ukraine, begun during the last century, continued largely unhindered. The extension of the Commonwealth's authority over the Ukraine was symbolised by the construction of a massive fort at Kodak, commanding the middle and lower reaches of the Dnieper River.

The onward march of the Commonwealth into the steppeland of the Ukraine and over Smolensk posed a formidable challenge to Muscovy (see map on page 33). On two sides the Russian state was hemmed in by the Polish advance. Moreover, the double thrust of Polish conquest suggested that in the long struggle for the mass of territory lying between the Baltic and the Black Sea, the Commonwealth was now emerging as the victorious power. Unless this trend could be arrested, Muscovy faced the prospect of being driven back into the forest fastnesses of the north.

During the second half of the seventeenth century, the tide of Polish expansion was strikingly reversed. Within the space of a few decades, Muscovy not only recaptured much of the land lost during the 'Time of Troubles' but rolled back the Polish settlement of the Ukraine. This momentous achievement owed much both to the Commonwealth's own domestic difficulties, and to the work of military reform undertaken by the Romanov Tsars. However, a significant contribution was also made by the Cossack inhabitants of the Ukraine. The Cossacks' rebellion against Polish rule gave Muscovy the opportunity it sought to intervene in the steppe-region and to replace Polish mastery there with one of its own.

The Cossack rebellion in the Ukraine was brought about by two separate factors. Firstly, as the Poles settled the region, they converted its free inhabitants into serfs, imposing on them obligations as onerous as those endured by their Muscovite counterparts. The process of enserfment bore heavily on the peasant smallholders and free Cossacks of the region. Many of these sought release either by fleeing to the 'land of the free communes' (that part of the steppe not yet subject to Polish colonisation) or by joining the Zaporozhian Host Cossack community. Still more responded by engaging in acts of rebellion against their landlords.

Secondly, the Polish landlords who established themselves in the Ukraine were in the main Catholics. By contrast, the majority of the inhabitants were of the orthodox faith. In the Union of Brest (1596), the Polish bishops sought to resolve these confessional differences by establishing a religious 'half-way house' known as the Uniate Church. The Uniate Church broadly adhered to orthodox ceremonies while also acknowledging the supremacy of the Pope in Rome. Although this new arrangement won some support in White Russia, it met with widespread popular disapproval in the Ukraine. Harsh measures, introduced by the Polish authorities to enforce acceptance of the Union, only added to the resistance gathering against Polish rule. As the Ukrainian *Chronicle of the Eye-Witness*, composed in the 1640s, tells, the inhabitants of the Ukraine were subjected to:

1 ... barbaric punishments for the least offences. Even children
have been killed and many a time our women and daughters have
been subject to abuse ... It would be bad enough if it was only
the squire who robbed us, but some wretched [agent of his] will
5 also enrich himself at our expense, invent various taxes for
orthodox weddings, impose a duty for christening children,
collect a levy for milling grain ... They force us to join the
Uniates and to sell the church plate.

* Throughout the early decades of the seventeenth century, popular opposition to Polish rule made itself felt in scattered uprisings. In 1647, however, a revolt of unprecedented proportions led by the Cossack Bohdan Khmelnitzky, swept the Ukraine. Khmelnitzky's motive for starting the rebellion was personal. Properties belonging to him in Volhynia had been taken unlawfully by a powerful landowner with friends at court and, despite his pleadings, Khmelnitzky was unable to obtain redress from the King. Khmelnitzky's predicament typified the insults suffered by the Ukrainians at the hands of their Polish overlords and elicited considerable sympathy. Khmelnitzky's eventual resort to arms in pursuit of his lost land thus rapidly acquired the character of a popular movement. Within the year, the Cossacks of the Zaporozhian Host had elected Khmelnitzky their commander or Hetman. This position gave him an added measure of personal authority as well as access to the Host's cannons and horsemen.

In a manifesto published in 1648, Khmelnitzky explained the circumstances which had led to his rebellion and called upon the orthodox community in the Ukraine to lend him assistance:

1 I have hitherto undertaken tasks which I had not thought
through; henceforth I shall pursue aims which I have considered
with great care. I shall free the entire people of the Ukraine from
the Poles. Up to now I have fought because of the wrongs done to
5 me personally; now I shall fight for our orthodox faith ... Not a
single prince or nobleman shall I permit to set foot in the
Ukraine, and if anyone desires to eat our bread he must be loyal
and obedient to the Zaporozhian Host. I am a small and
insignificant man, but by the will of God I have become the
10 independent ruler of the Ukraine.

* Khmelnitzky's rebellion depended for success upon foreign support, for he had insufficient resources to defy the Poles for long. Orthodox Muscovy, which had earlier suffered losses at the hands of

The Statue of Bohdan Khmelnitzky now in the centre of Kiev

In the old times all this country, now called Little Russia, had its own rulers, till it was subjected by the Poles, who have ever since exercised cruel tyranny upon it . . . But God raised Khmelnitzky to punish them and to deliver his people from slavery . . .

The Diary of the Travels of Patriarch Macarius of Antioch, 1653–60

In Ukrainian history [Khmelnitzky] appears as a pioneer of national liberation. In Soviet Russia, he is remembered as a Moses who led his people's exodus from Polish bondage towards the great Russian homeland. In the Valhalla of Marxist and sociological heroes, he is presented as a champion of social conscience and protest. He was none of these things. He harboured a deep, personal and understandable grudge against [Jeremy] Wisniowiecki, whose men had assaulted his property; and he gravitated towards the [Host] as the natural haven for all such fugitives and malcontents. Then, having failed to obtain redress by his initial resort to force, he had no alternative but to fight to the end. Otherwise, he would have been hanged as a traitor.

Norman Davies, *God's Playground. A History of Poland* (Oxford University Press, 1981) the Poles, was seen as a ready and obvious source of support. Unfortunately for the Cossacks, Tsar Alexey had ambitions of his own in the Ukraine, a region which he considered on historical grounds rightfully to belong to Muscovy.

In 1654 the Cossacks agreed that Alexey should take the Ukraine under his 'protection'. In return, they would lend him military support in the war he was preparing against the Poles. The alliance served both parties well. The Poles were rapidly put to flight and Smolensk together with the whole region around Seversk and Chernigov was captured. However, these early successes soon gave way to calamity, when Charles X of Sweden entered the contest and invaded Poland (his motives are discussed on page 77). Charles's advance through Poland was so rapid and unexpected as to upset the entire balance of power in eastern Europe. In terror of the new invader from the north, Poland and Muscovy put aside their differences and forged a common front against the Swedes.

Had the Cossacks remained united, they might have exploited the turmoil brought about by the Swedish irruption into eastern Europe. However in 1657, Hetman Khmelnitzky died. A prolonged struggle for supremacy then ensued between the various Cossack communities. This made them an easy target for attack.

Khmelnitzky's death was followed three years later by that of Charles X. Thereupon, the Swedes withdrew from Poland. With their common enemy now departed, both Poland and Muscovy resumed their struggle for the Ukraine. Owing to Poland's growing internal difficulties, Muscovy gained the upper hand in this phase of the conflict. In the Truce of Andrusovo, sealed in 1667, Poland and Muscovy partitioned the Ukraine along the River Dnieper. While the western portion of the Ukraine was returned to Poland, the eastern parts together with the city of Kiev were assigned to Muscovy. For the time being, the Zaporozhian Host was permitted a shadowy and ill-defined independence under the continued rule of its elected Hetmans.

The diplomatic settlement was followed by a process of administrative and social reorganisation. The agents of Polish and Muscovite government installed themselves on both sides of the Dnieper, and military garrisons were imposed on the countryside. In their wake came the colonisers, parcelling the land into agricultural units and enserfing peasants and Cossacks alike. Continued outbreaks of rebellion did little to halt the steady progress of subjugation.

4 The Polish Deluge

In 1632, the newly-elected King of Poland, Wladyslaw IV, attended his first meeting with the *Seym*. Eager to view the occasion, one of the Queen's ladies-in-waiting leaned too far over the rail of the spectators' gallery. The balustrade gave way and the lady fell forward into the vault of the chamber. In the descent, her dress caught and held fast on a nail. The nail saved her life, but not her dignity. With much ripping and tearing, the lady's garments unravelled, leaving her suspended in mid-air, held up above the astonished deputies by only the slender strand of clothing left around her waist.

This unusual event may be considered a metaphor of the history of Poland–Lithuania during the seventeenth century. The political organization and stability of the Commonwealth depended upon an equilibrium being achieved between the diverging interests of crown, magnates and *Seym*. Over the course of the century, this precarious balance was lost. Rather like the lady in the story, the Commonwealth was plunged headlong into chaos, and its constitution unravelled. Rapidly stripped of its dignity and poise, the Commonwealth soon became an object of astonishment among the powers of Europe, not least on account of its evident vulnerability and distress.

A principal cause of Poland's 'ruin' lay in its transformation from a 'commonwealth of the nobles' to a 'commonwealth of a few of the greatest nobles'. During the last decades of the sixteenth century, a new generation of magnates emerged in Poland far wealthier in land and resources than any of their predecessors. By taking advantage of the high demand for Polish grain in Europe, these magnates acquired massive spreads of *latifundia*. They bought out their neighbours and even took over small towns. Although the pattern of landownership differed widely from place to place, Lithuania had the greatest concentration of large estates. The spectacular and rapid growth of magnate landholding is amply demonstrated by the examples of Jan Zamoyski and Jeremy Wisniowiecki. In 1572, Zamoyski owned a mere four villages; by the close of the century his properties included some 200 villages and 11 towns. Between 1630 and 1647 the Wisniowiecki estates grew sixtyfold in size, eventually incorporating a population of almost a quarter of a milion.

The magnates dominated not only the Senate and the principal court offices but the political life of the countryside as well. Their courts and palaces provided a focus for the ambitions of the poorer nobles, who entered their service as clients and household retainers. As the diminutive Joseph Boruwlaski explained in his *Memoirs of a Celebrated Dwarf* (London, 1788):

1 'Tis a custom in Poland for the lords . . . to take young persons of good birth, who are brought up at their own charge, and afterwards provided for, either by admitting them into their household, giving them in marriage, or procuring them civil or
5 military employments. This ancient custom has its origin in the wide disproportion of fortunes among the nobility.

As the magnates' powers of local patronage grew, so their placemen came to dominate the *seymiks*. Through control of the *seymiks*, the great lords were able to influence the selection of deputies to the *Seym* and ensure that this body enacted no legislation harmful to their interests. The *liberum veto* provided a convenient device for upsetting the passage of laws, and during the second half of the century was used much less sparingly than before. In 1652 the *Seym* was 'broken' for the first time by use of the *veto*. A single shout, delivered by a client nobleman on behalf of his patron, rendered void all the business conducted over the preceding weeks. In 1668 the cry of *Nie pozwalam* ('I forbid it') was heard even on the opening day of the *Seym*.

Against the growing power of the magnates the crown was increasingly helpless. The influence of the magnates permeated every level of Polish society, and they and their agents dominated central and local government. All attempts by the Kings of Poland to retrieve their authority only served to make their position all the more beleaguered. Fearful lest any 'foreign absolutism' be introduced, many former supporters of the crown deserted its ranks and threw in their lot with the magnates.

* The 'Polish Deluge' (1648–68) was released by Bohdan Khmelnitzky. His rebellion in the Ukraine had been rapidly transformed into a war between Poland and Muscovy, with the Cossacks supporting the latter. The fall of Smolensk and King John Casimir of Poland's apparent inability to halt the foreign advance, had caused panic among the magnates. In order to protect their estates against invasion, the leader of the Lithuanian magnates (Janusz Radziwill) had begged the help of Charles X of Sweden (see page 75).

Charles X was himself related to John Casimir, for ever since the late sixteenth century the Kings of Poland had been selected from among the Catholic branch of the Swedish royal house of Vasa. The two lines of the Vasa family were bitter rivals and both nursed personal and political grievances against the other. During the reign of Charles X's illustrious predecessor, Gustavus Adolphus (1611–32), Sweden had overrun the Polish province of Livonia and had for a short time occupied the Polish ports on the Baltic coast.

Charles enthusiastically welcomed the magnates' invitation and promptly invaded Poland. For six years, Swedish troops roamed the Polish countryside, sacking the cities and plundering the land. Military interventions by Transylvanian, Habsburg and Tatar forces added to the confusion, and the Duke of Prussia took the opportunity to declare his duchy independent of the Polish crown. During this period of the 'Deluge', the urban population of Poland is reckoned to have declined by 70 per cent and most of the country's arable land is thought to have lain fallow. Although the estates of the great lords suffered enormously during these years, their retinues were swollen by a great influx of nobles seeking help and protection.

In 1660 Charles X died and peace was made between Poland and

Sweden. Shortly afterwards, John Casimir published plans to convert the Commonwealth into a hereditary monarchy and to abolish the *liberum veto*. The response to this attempt at rebuilding the authority of the crown was predictable. In 1665 a group of magnates raised the standard of revolt. With the support of a large body of *szlachta*, they defeated the royal forces in 1667, thereby compelling the King's abdication the next year.

The experience of the 'Deluge' did not lead to any reform of the constitution, still less to any attempt to root out the underlying causes of Polish decay. During the reigns of John Casimir's successors, the power of the magnates continued to grow, the authority of the crown shrank further, and both *szlachta* and *Seym* ceased to play any significant role in the Commonwealth's affairs. Even the election in 1674 of a shrewd, native king, Jan Sobieski, failed to halt the creeping paralysis which affected the public life of the country. Despite the tremendous prestige he accumulated in his wars against the Turks, all Sobieski's plans for reform were vetoed.

In this unrelieved condition of decay, the Commonwealth lingered on as a 'beautifully phosphorescent rot-heap' (Thomas Carlyle), quite unprepared for the challenges of the next century. As a consequence of its internal weakness, the Commonwealth had already been obliged to cede half of the Ukraine to its Muscovite neighbour, now fully recovered from its own 'Time of Troubles'. In the years which followed, Russian influence would continue to increase at the expense of Polish independence and sovereignty, until by the end of the eighteenth century, Poland quite simply ceased to exist.

Making notes on 'The Seventeenth Century'

This chapter focuses on three separate crises: the 'Time of Troubles' in Muscovy; the Khmelnitzky Revolt in the Ukraine; and the 'Polish Deluge'. Each of these three episodes is examined in its wider context and various conclusions are drawn as to historical developments in Muscovy, Poland and the Ukraine. When reading this chapter, you should not concentrate on the details of each particular crisis. You should be thinking about what these different crises tell you about conditions and problems in each of the regions affected. In making notes, the following headings, sub-headings and questions should help you:
1. The Muscovite 'Time of Troubles'
1.1. Platonov's 'three phases'
1.2. The 'dynastic phase'
     Tsar Fedor

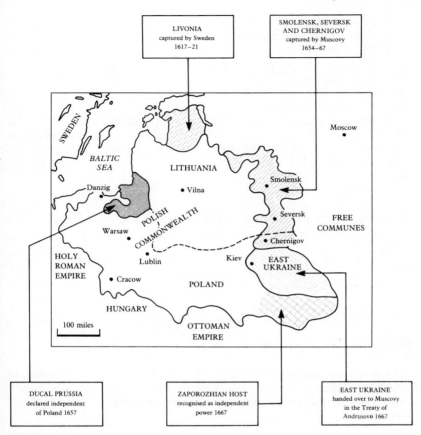

Polish territorial losses, 1617–67

Boris Godunov
Dmitri–Otrepev and Basil Shuisky
1.3. The 'social phase'. The plight of the peasantry. Why was the flight of the peasantry considered so potentially damaging as to justify the introduction of serfdom?
1.4. The phase of 'national struggle'
Polish and Swedish intervention
The militias
The election of Michael Romanov. How might the circumstances under which Michael was appointed Tsar have put his government on a firmer footing than that of his immediate predecessors?
2. The Romanov recovery

Why, when his predecessors had largely sought to avoid war, did Tsar Alexey willingly enter into an armed struggle with the Poles for possession of the Ukraine?

How did Poland's internal troubles deepen and prolong the crisis caused by Khmelnitzky's revolt in the Ukraine?

Answering essay questions on 'The Seventeenth Century'

Questions on this period of east European history normally relate to Muscovite affairs. Nevertheless, certain types of question will require you to refer also to developments in contemporary Poland and the Ukraine:

1. 'What was the contribution of the Tsars Michael and Alexey Romanov to the strengthening and development of Muscovy in the seventeenth century?'

2. 'How may Russia's rapid recovery from the "Time of Troubles" be explained?'

Both these questions involve above all a consideration of the achievements of the first Romanov Tsars. In composing your answer, you will need to draw attention to their domestic reforms and initiatives, and to their work of administrative and military reform. Muscovy's territorial growth and consolidation during Alexey's reign owed much, however, to Polish weakness and to the opportunity presented by the Cossack revolt. In discussing foreign policy, therefore, you would be right to consider briefly Poland's internal difficulties and the situation in the Ukraine, both of which facilitated Russian expansion over this period.

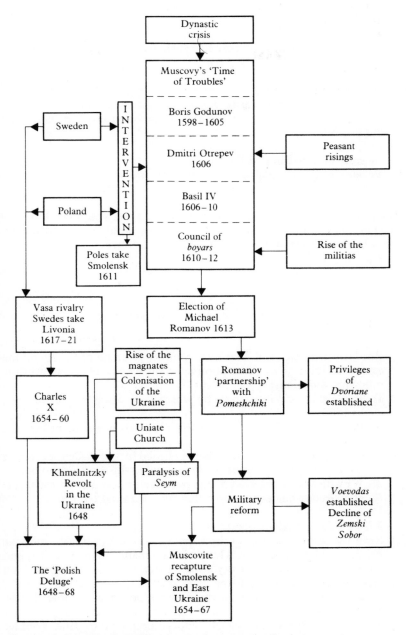

Russia, Poland and the Ukraine in the seventeenth century

The 'Time of Troubles' sometimes merits a question in its own right on A-level papers.

3. 'Why did Muscovy experience such grave internal disorder in the period 1598–1613?'

In approaching any type of question beginning with a 'Why?', you should begin by constructing a plan consisting of short statements starting with 'Because . . .' In the case of the question given here, you might choose:

Because of Swedish and Polish involvement
Because of the worsening condition of the peasantry
Because of the absence of a legitimate Tsar.

What other points would you add to this list? How would you build up each of these points so as to make a single paragraph? What information would you use to support the point you are making?

Source-based questions on 'The Seventeenth Century'

1 Tsar Basil IV
Read the declaration of Tsar Basil Shuisky given on page 65, and the extract taken from a contemporary chronicle on page 65. Answer the following questions:
a) Explain the circumstances by which Basil Shuisky became Tsar in 1606.
b) How does Basil attempt to justify his newly-acquired position as Tsar?
c) To what extent are Basil's claims refuted by the evidence given in the chronicle? How reliable do you judge this evidence to be?
d) Why do both these documents put such importance on the terms and circumstances by which the ruler acquired the throne?

2 The Khmelnitzky Revolt
Read the account given by the *Chronicle of the Eye-Witness* on page 73, the extract taken from Khmelnitzky's manifesto on page 73, and the opinions of Khmelnitzky's role, together with the picture, on page 74. Answer the following questions:
a) Explain the reference to the Uniates on page 73, line 8 (first extract)?
b) What religious and social factors combined to lend popular support to Khmelnitzky's revolt?

c) Using the explanation given by Norman Davies, consider why a statue in Khmelnitzky's honour may be found today in the capital city of the Soviet Ukraine.

d) On the basis of the evidence contained in the two accounts given by Khmelnitzky and Patriarch Macarius, explain whether you believe Khmelnitzky's revolt to have been inspired by personal, religious or nationalistic motives.

CHAPTER 5

Peter the Great and Russia

1 Interpreting Peter the Great

The *Plain Dealer*, an English newspaper of the early eighteenth century, was hardly exaggerating when it described Peter I of Russia (1682–1725) as, 'the greatest monarch of our age . . . whose actions will draw after him a blaze of glory and astonishment, through the latest depth of time'. For contemporaries and historians alike, the reign of Peter the Great amounted to a turning-point in Russian history, made all the more momentous by the stupendous personal qualities of the ruler who brought about this change. Under Peter's direction, Muscovy embraced the west and sought to transform itself into a modern, European state. The reforms undertaken during Peter's reign affected every aspect of Muscovy's government and society and their legacy may be felt even to this day.

Much of Peter's reputation derives from the astonishing variety of his activities and achievements. This feature of his rule has allowed different generations and shades of opinion to interpret his place in history very much according to their own tastes. For many nineteenth-century liberals, therefore, Peter led Russia out of the darkness of superstition and tradition into the light of reason. For their conservative counterparts, Peter's reign served as an example of the benefits of autocratic government. In Stalin's opinion, Peter the Great was his own precursor, engaged like himself in prising Russia 'out of the framework of backwardness'.

Despite these differences of viewpoint, contemporaries and historians are agreed in one respect: throughout his reign Peter consistently endeavoured to make Muscovy a part of Europe. His work of reform thus assumed the character of 'westernisation', as he deliberately imposed on his subjects new European methods of government, and of military, technical and social organization. Cutting off the boyars' beards and making the nobility adopt western dress are marvellous illustrations of Peter's breadth of purpose, made all the more telling by their apparent triviality. Equally symbolic is Peter's construction of a new capital city on the Gulf of Finland. The site chosen for the city of St Petersburg epitomises Peter's desire to reorientate Russia towards the west and to give his empire 'a great window . . . looking into Europe'.

By any measure, Peter's reign was a decisive epoch in Russian history. Yet although the extent of Peter's achievement cannot be doubted, the character of his achievement has undergone substantial reassessment over recent decades. Nowadays, few scholars would agree with Chaadeyev's estimate: 'Peter the Great found at home in Russia only a blank sheet of paper. With his powerful hand he wrote on it "Europe and the West"'. In particular, historians have pointed out that Peter's hand was held by circumstance and that the script in which he wrote was uneven. Nor was Russia by any means a 'blank sheet of paper'. Thanks to the work of Peter's predecessors, Russia already had 'Europe and the West' printed firmly upon it. Peter's work of transformation rested upon the achievements of others, and his reign demonstrates elements of continuity as well as of change.

2 'Westernisation' before Peter

At no time in its history was Russia ever 'severed' from the rest of Europe, for even during the grim years of the Mongol–Tatar yoke, Muscovy had managed to preserve some patchy contact with the west. These tenuous relations were established on a firmer and lasting basis during the fifteenth century when Ivan III opened up new diplomatic and commercial channels to the west. By the close of Ivan's reign, Italian architects were redesigning the Kremlin walls and adding their own ornate friezes to Moscow's onion-domed churches. A few decades later, individual boyars were even shaving their beards, donning extravagant ruffs, and apeing in their dress the dandies of the French court.

Despite these interchanges, Muscovite attitudes towards the rest of Europe were founded largely on suspicion and contempt. Muscovites were convinced that theirs was the wisest, most intelligently governed and most sophisticated nation upon earth, and that they stood in no need of foreign advice. As Ivan IV dismissively wrote to Elizabeth of England, 'We had thought that you were sovereign in your state and ruled yourself . . . But it turns out that in your land people rule besides you, and not just people, but merchant peasants . . .'.

* Muscovy's confidence in its own self-sufficiency evaporated during the seventeenth century. The growing commerce with the rest of Europe revealed the technical inadequacies of Russian manufacture and war exposed Muscovy's military backwardness. Expansion into the Ukraine led in its turn to the discovery there of the fruits of Catholic learning and scholarship. Through this medium of transmission came the earliest Russian stage plays, works of secular literature, and examples of Baroque architecture. Seeds of self-doubt were even sown within the highly traditionalist ecclesiastical establishment. During Alexey's reign, many of the old liturgical texts on which the church based its ceremonies, were examined afresh and rejected as flawed. A scholarly review of the ancient written sources of the orthodox faith led to a 'reformation' in religious practices and provoked a schism in the church between 'modernisers' and Old Believers. A particular com-

plaint of the Old Believers was the replacement of the old styles of icon painting by new techniques of representation borrowed from western Europe.

The court in Moscow, as the principal gathering place for visiting merchants, soldiers and diplomats, provided an important channel through which western ideas and inspiration flowed. During the regency of Princess Sophie (1682–89), the ballet, theatre, rose-garden and library became established forms of entertainment and relaxation among the élite of society. In the palace of Sophie's lover, Prince Golitsyn, mirrors, clocks, European furniture and paintings vied for space, while noble womenfolk (hitherto confined to silence and back-rooms) conversed with western diplomats.

By the last decades of the seventeenth century, leading sections of Muscovite society had already made the intellectual leap from the traditionalism of the past to the new world of western ideas. Their growing admiration for all things European and their willingness to learn from the west, provided the background and springboard for Peter the Great's own work of reform.

3 The 'Great Embassy' to the West

Peter's early years were attended by a struggle for power, and there was nothing inevitable about his eventual accession. Following the death without heir of Tsar Alexey's eldest son, Fedor II (1676–82), the crown should have passed to Alexey's second son, Ivan. However, he was crippled and dim-witted and thus the unprecedented decision was taken to have Ivan share the throne with his younger brother, Peter. Since Peter was only nine at the time, a regency was declared under his sister, the Princess Sophie. However, Sophie herself had designs on the throne and had no wish to concede power to her brother when he came of age. Throughout his boyhood and youth, therefore, Peter was kept in seclusion away from Moscow.

Peter was not idle during his years of isolation, demonstrating a precocious enthusiasm for military affairs. An arsenal, parade-ground, and even a regiment were provided for his amusement, and the young Tsar began to take lessons in warfare. On one occasion, he chanced upon the hulk of an Elizabethan sailing-boat lying neglected in a storehouse. Quite how and why this vessel should have reached Muscovy remains uncertain. Nevertheless, the mysterious ship fired Peter's imagination. His passion later on in life for building up a war-fleet may be traced back to this boyhood encounter. Fittingly, the ship he found and which he later named 'the grandfather of the Russian navy', is today a prized exhibit in the Leningrad Naval Museum.

Adolescence gave way to manhood and Peter still lingered in busy seclusion, seemingly content to leave the work of government to the ambitious Sophie. Neither his marriage nor occasional visits to the court induced in Peter any desire to play a more active role in politics. Sophie, however, was wary of her brother and feared him as a potential focus of opposition to her rule. Eventually in 1689, her nerve gave way and she made a clumsy attempt to have Peter arrested. This led to a tussle for the reins of government. As the legitimate ruler, Peter was able to rally sufficient support from the army to ensure his sister's overthrowal. With his position and inheritance thus secured, he resumed his isolation, transferring the government of the country to his mother. During this period, Peter spent much time in the foreign quarter of Moscow, conversing and carousing with visiting merchants, soldiers and seamen. He eagerly questioned them about western innovations in science and technology and showed a profound interest in all that they had to say.

* This prolonged period of apparent self-indulgence came to an end in the mid-1690s. The death of Peter's mother in 1694 was followed shortly afterwards by the decease of his brother. This double-loss left Peter the sole ruler of Muscovy in deed as well as in title, and emphasised his personal responsibility for the country's government. Peter's response to these changed circumstances was to employ his military education in 'the real game' (as he put it). In 1695 a Muscovite army, borne by a flotilla of barges, advanced down the River Don. The next year, the Turkish fort and city of Azov fell. If Peter could follow up this victory by seizing the Straits of Kerch, the Black Sea would be opened up to his warships and merchants. For this, however, he would need the help of other European powers, for the Turks were bound to resist the extension of Muscovite influence into the Black Sea.

* Shortly after the fall of Azov, Peter announced that he intended to leave the country and to travel to western Europe. The motives behind this extraordinary decision (for no Tsar had ever before journeyed abroad) were clear. Peter wished to make personal contact with other European rulers in the hope of winning their support for a coalition against the Ottoman Turks. He was also anxious to see for himself the fruits of western technological progress about which he had heard so much.

With a retinue of 250 men, Peter left Moscow in March 1697 and travelled westwards by way of Livonia and north Germany. He wintered in the United Provinces and spent the spring and early summer of 1698 in England. Peter had intended to pass through Europe largely *incognito*. However, news of the Tsar's 'Great Embassy' and of his own enormous size (he was almost seven feet tall) ensured him speedy recognition and a series of lavish receptions. During one such entertainment in Hanover, he felt with astonishment the abdomen of his dancing partner, believing her hard whalebone corset to be her rib-cage; mostly, however, Peter directed his investigations to more inanimate objects. In Prussia he underwent a course in gunnery and proudly received a certificate attesting to his good progress. At

Zaandam in Holland he made a piece of paper with his own hands and toiled in the shipyards. In Amsterdam he attended anatomy classes and looked down a microscope.

From Holland, Peter crossed the Channel to Portsmouth, whence he made his way to London. In one famous incident, his entourage wrecked the house they were in, using the furniture for firewood, the pictures for target-practice, and the garden for wheel-barrow races. Although he joined in these sports, Peter also engaged in more weighty business. He attended the royal court and the House of Lords, and visited museums and factories. Much of his time was spent in the dockyards, where he toiled to learn the craft of shipbuilding, a pastime which elicited much surprise. As the imperial ambassador wrote to the Emperor in Vienna:

1   All the time he went about in sailor's clothing. We shall see in
    what dress he presents himself to Your Imperial Majesty. He saw
    the King [William III] very rarely, as he did not wish to change
    his manner of life . . . They say that he intends to civilize his
5   subjects in the manner of other nations. But from his actions
    here, one cannot find any other intention than to make them
    sailors.

A less condescending opinion was provided by the Bishop of Salisbury, with whom Peter had several conversations:

1   He is a man of very hot temper, soon influenced, and very brutal
    in his passion . . . He is subject to convulsive motions all over his
    body and his head seems to be affected with these. He wants not
    capacity, and has a larger measure of knowledge than might be
5   expected from his education, which was very indifferent; a want
    of judgement and an instability of temper appear in him too often
    and too evidently. He is mechanically turned, and seems designed
    by nature rather to be a ship's carpenter than a great prince. This
    was his chief study and exercise while he stayed here. He wrought
10 much with his own hands, and made all about him work at the
    models of ships . . . He was indeed resolved to encourage
    learning, and to polish his people by sending some of them to
    travel in other countries, and to draw strangers to come and live
    among them . . . After I had seen him, I could not but admire the
15 depth of the providence of God, that had raised up such a furious
    man to so absolute authority over so great a part of the world.

4 The Impact of War

Peter travelled back to Muscovy by way of Vienna where he had lengthy discussions concerning his proposed coalition against the Turks. However, neither here nor elsewhere were Peter's diplomatic plans taken seriously. He was too curious a figure, and too unknown a quantity, to be regarded as an ally. Despite this failure, Peter's 'Great Embassy' to western Europe had stirred within him a desire to seek Muscovy's modernisation and transformation. Thus, once returned to Moscow, he at once sought to impose western manners on his subjects, beginning by ordering the boyars to shave off their beards and to dress in western attire. Under Peter's cajoling and personal example, the new customs soon spread to distant outposts of the administration, exciting the following comment from the British ambassador in Turkey:

1 The Muscovite ambassador and his retinue have appeared here so different from what they formerly wore that the Turks cannot tell what to make of them. They are all [dressed] in French habit, with an abundance of gold and silver lace, long *perruques* and,
5 which the Turks most wonder at, without beards. Last Sunday, being at mass in Adrianople, the ambassador and all his company did not only keep all their hats off during the whole ceremony, but at the elevation himself and all of them pulled off their wigs. It was much taken note of and thought an unusual act of
10 devotion.

On his return to Muscovy Peter also ordered a reform of the Russian calendar, so as to bring it into line with the method of dating followed in western Europe, and commanded that the coinage be restruck after the fashion of London's Royal Mint. Shortly afterwards, Peter drew up the earliest plans for the new capital at St Petersburg. Construction of the city was begun in 1703 under the supervision of an Italian architect.

The process of westernisation inaugurated by these measures gathered pace during the first years of the new century. In 1700 Peter commenced hostilities against Sweden, thereby committing Muscovy to the Great Northern War and to a struggle which was to last for 19 years. As it turned out, Muscovy was grievously unprepared for the war which followed. A basic lack of resources, combined with poor military provision and administrative disorganization made Muscovy an easy prey for invasion. In order to meet the Swedish challenge, Peter was forced to increase the tempo of modernisation. However, under the strain of war, the changes he introduced were piecemeal rather than systematic. As a consequence, Muscovy's westernisation proved more uneven and superficial than might have been the case had it been undertaken during peace-time.

* At the outbreak of war, Peter's most pressing task was to expand and improve the quality of his army. In 1698 Muscovy's regular forces comprised 30000 troops, organized in 27 infantry and 2 dragoon regiments. In November 1700, at the Battle of Narva, this army was

routed amidst total confusion in the ranks. As one eye-witness reported, 'They ran about like a herd of cattle, one regiment got mixed up with the other, so that hardly 20 men could be got in line'. To replace the army lost at Narva, Peter rapidly raised an additional 60 regiments. This prodigious effort continued at an unrelenting pace over the ensuing years. By 1711 Peter's regular army consisted of no less than 160 000 men, supported by about 100 000 Cossacks and auxiliaries.

The war against Sweden was partly fought at sea, and this aspect of the struggle gave Peter a fresh incentive to develop the Muscovite navy. Expenditure on shipbuilding soared from 81 thousand roubles in 1701 to 1.2 million roubles by 1724. By the end of Peter's reign the Baltic fleet consisted of 34 ships-of-the-line and 15 frigates, and was reckoned more powerful than the navies of either Sweden or Denmark. Only on a few occasions, however, was Peter able to use his navy and its development owed more to personal fancy than to any pressing national need. For this reason, the Russian navy went into rapid decline after Peter's death.

* The hasty expansion of the Muscovite armed forces, and the victory they ultimately gained against the Swedes, depended upon adequate manpower, training and resources. These three preconditions of military success could only be met by the radical reorganization of Muscovite society. In the main, Peter's regiments were made up of peasants drawn from the countryside. Although at first Peter tried to man his army with volunteers, conscription to the ranks was the usual method of recruitment. Every 20 peasant households were ordered to provide a fit and healthy young man for 25 years' military service. The conscript was trained in modern methods of warfare, taught to fire on command, and instructed in use of the bayonet. Until Muscovy was capable of its own arms manufacture, flintlock muskets were imported from England for the conscript's use. A generous wage and a simple green uniform with tricorn hat completed the peasant's transformation into a disciplined, well-equipped and loyal trooper.

* The dependence of the Muscovite army on a foreign officer corps was considered by Peter to be both demeaning and unnecessary. As he exclaimed early on in his reign, 'Why should I spend money on foreigners when my own subjects can do as well as they?' The truth was that unless they were properly trained, native officers were no match for mercenary captains recruited from abroad. The establishment of military academies, begun in 1698, represented a first step in the creation of an efficient and reliable body of Muscovite officers. However, the poor state of educational provision in Muscovy meant that many of those sent for military training were ill prepared for any form of advanced study. To remedy this deficiency, Peter was obliged to provide elementary education for the sons of the nobility and to have them taught reading, writing, arithmetic and geometry. In order to compel attendance at the new schools, Peter laid down that no young

nobleman was entitled to marry until he had obtained a certificate attesting to his numerical proficiency.

Lack of money, an absence of teachers, and the nobility's traditional distaste for academic pursuits limited the success of Peter's programme of educational reform. Nevertheless, the production of new textbooks and grammars, and the conversion to Arabic numerals, laid the foundation of educational provision in Muscovy. On this achievement, Peter's successors would build. More importantly, native officers were educated and trained in sufficient numbers to take the place of their foreign counterparts in the army. Whereas at the start of Peter's reign, almost a half of the commissioned ranks had consisted of mercenaries from abroad, by the 1720s they amounted to less than an eighth.

* Before Peter's accession Muscovy had little industry or manufacture. As a consequence, many raw materials, gunpowder, arms, sailcloth, and even material for uniforms, had to be imported. With the outbreak of the Great Northern War, Peter urgently set about making his country economically self-sufficient. To that end, he invited in Dutch and German engineers to build new ironworks and foundries and undertook the construction of textile mills himself. The extent of Peter's economic achievement may be measured by the growth in the number of industrial enterprises from about 20 in the 1680s to over 200 by the 1720s. Although the country lagged far behind western Europe in terms of output, a favourable balance of trade with the outside world had been obtained by the time of Peter's death. Most importantly, however, Muscovy was now producing its own artillery and muskets, and mixing its own gunpowder.

5 Finance and Administration

Peter himself recognised that 'the artery of war is money', and his reign was punctuated by feverish attempts to find new sources of revenue for his armies. The introduction of a tax on beards, of duties payable on weddings and taverns, and the sale of high-sounding but meaningless honours attest to an ingenuity borne of desperate need.

Only in 1718 did Peter attempt to put his revenues on a firm and uniform footing when he introduced a poll tax or, as it was quaintly known 'a tax on souls'. A census of the population was taken, and on the basis of the returns, all non-nobles were made to contribute an annual sum for the upkeep of the army. The business of listing 'souls' and of collecting the tax, required unprecedented bureaucratic effort and volumes of paperwork. In 1724 a central register was compiled in Moscow, which gave details of every landowner in the country and of how many serfs he owned. The soul tax proved the most successful of Peter's financial innovations and led to a threefold increase in state revenues. The registration of the tax-paying population also aided military enlistment by enabling the government to keep a record of potential recruits.

* The soul tax accelerated the trend towards bureaucracy and detailed regulation. As early as 1701, Peter had introduced proper methods of accounting in the chanceries, which were at that time the principal instruments of Muscovite government. In 1710–11, a state budget was prepared (far in advance of most western countries), so that Peter could monitor income and expenditure more closely. Despite these improvements, the central and local government of Muscovy remained too cumbersome and antiquated to perform its tasks adequately. Chanceries jostled for influence and the *voevodas* in the countryside remained impervious to direction. Conflict rather than co-operation marked the relationship between the various branches of the administration, upsetting and hindering the work of financial reform.

The local administration was the first branch of government to undergo substantial reorganization. Between 1708 and 1710 the *voevodas* lost many of their powers, and the country was divided into eight enormous 'governments' or *gubernii*. A governor enjoying full civil and military authority was established over each of these areas. The principal motive behind this reform was to speed up the process of decision-making in the countryside, for local initiative was frequently thwarted by the need to refer for advice to distant Moscow. Since, however, the new areas of government were still too large to be effectively administered, the system never worked satisfactorily. In 1718, the structure was drastically reshaped and local units of administration headed by *voevodas* and military commissioners were introduced.

Much of the inspiration for Peter's reform of local government derived from the example of Sweden, whose administration Peter subjected to close personal scrutiny. In much the same way, he used foreign models to help him reshape the central institutions of government. The system of colleges introduced in 1718 was also based heavily on Swedish practices. The colleges were in effect departments of state, organized by function, and were designed to supersede the cumbersome chancery administration. There were 11 (later 12) colleges altogether, those of foreign affairs, war and the admiralty being prominent.

The ministers or presidents of the colleges were in their turn made responsible to a central administrative body, the Senate. Originally established in 1711 to stand in for the Tsar when he was on campaign, the Senate gradually acquired a permanent character. The nine senators collectively held supreme administrative, judicial and financial authority in the state, under the Tsar. A corps of 500 'supervisors' or *fiskals* was responsible to the Senate for hunting out corruption and mismanagement in all branches of the administration.

* The rationalization of government was accompanied by a rationalization of society. Behind the soul tax lay the basic idea that Muscovy consisted of only two classes: non-nobles who paid tax, and nobles who served the Tsar in person and were therefore tax-exempt. During the 1720s, Peter published a 'Table of Ranks' which defined the services of the nobles more exactly. All noble office-holders in the court, in the administration and in the army were put in one of 14 categories, arranged hierarchically. The rank of each office-holder depended on the service he performed and the responsibilities he discharged. The higher the rank obtained by promotion, the greater the social prestige and more magnificent the title attaching to it. An annex published together with the Table of Ranks further explained that the right to hold land and to employ serf-labour depended on rank, which might only be obtained by the commitment to lifetime service.

Like the changes in the administration, the Table of Ranks borrowed heavily from foreign practices: in this case from the Prussian *Rangordnung* of 1713. The influence of the Table on the Muscovite nobility was similar to the effect of the *Rangordnung* on the Prussian *junkers* (nobles). As a consequence of its introduction, the Muscovite *dvoriane* were 'militarised' and made into the regimented servants of the state. Whether put to work in the army or in the administration, all nobles were subjected to the same system of command, hierarchy and promotion. The 'intermarriage of army and state', characteristic of Prussian militarism, was thus also accomplished in Muscovy, and at much the same time. During Peter's reign, Russia took on in this way the characteristic later defined by De Custine as its most salient and abiding: the permeation of its government and society by the discipline and mentality of the army camp.

6 The Church

The orthodox church had always held a position of respect and reverence in Muscovite society. Its influence and prestige were embodied in the office of patriarch, who as the head of the Muscovite church was considered the Tsar's spiritual counterpart. One German scholar, who visited Moscow in the 1630s, made the following comment on the powers attaching to the patriarch:

> 1 The Patriarch's authority is so great that he in manner divides sovereignty with the [Tsar]. He is the supreme judge of all the ecclesiastical cases, and absolutely disposes of whatever concerns religion, with such power that in things relating to the political
> 5 government, he reforms what he conceives prejudicial to Christian simplicity and good manners without giving the Tsar any account of it, who without any contestation commands the orders made by the patriarch to be executed.

Chanceries and Colleges

View of the 'Twelve Colleges' in St Petersburg. Designed by D. Trezzini (1722–42)

The central executive administration consisted of a motley network of chanceries, or so-called *prikazy*. There was no systematic division of jurisdiction between these organs . . . When a new need arose a *prikaz* was created to meet it, and when it had been met the *prikaz* in question was disbanded. Thus the number of administrative units was flexible and constantly changing. It has been calculated that 80 different *prikazy* existed at one time or another during the seventeenth century, of which approximately 40 were permanent, while many lasted only a few years. What is more, it was often difficult to draw any clear boundaries between the areas of jurisdiction of the various chanceries.

Claes Peterson, *Peter the Great's Administrative and Judicial Reforms: Swedish Antecedents and the Process of Reception* (Stockholm, 1979)

God, as a God of order, rules everything wisely and in an orderly manner with his invisible hand. The gods of this world, or the likenesses of God's power . . . have to establish their forms of government in accordance with this order if they wish to enjoy the sweet fruits of a flowering state for their great efforts . . . Experience has hitherto shown conclusively that realms and countries cannot be put in better order than through the establishment of good colleges . . .

Memorandum (undated, unsigned) to Peter the Great, c. 1713

[The colleges] are all organized on the Swedish model, in spite of the fact that they still have not brought any complete clarity in their work, since they do not have a good foundation, and no able men who understand the duties, although there is such a division in each college that the councillors or assessors are half of them Russians, and the other half foreigners.

The Swedish ambassador at St Petersburg, 1729

* In contrast to his predecessors, Peter demonstrated a profound contempt for churchmen. In the 1690s he founded his notorious drinking club, the Most Drunken Council. Not only did the name of this club deliberately recall the church's own Most Holy Council, but its members' garb was a mockery of clerical vestments. A 'patriarch' led the club's festivities, wearing . . .

1 . . . a costume made in facetious form, not the least bit like the [real] patriarch's; his mitre was of tin and was engraved with the figure of Bacchus [the god of wine] stuck in a cask, which was also sewn on the costumes of his retinue; similarly in place of pectoral
5 crosses they wore earthenware jugs . . . And in place of the Bible they made a book in which they carried several flasks of vodka.

According to this same writer, meetings of this Council were accompanied with 'much drunkenness, lechery and debauchery of every kind'. Peter had the club make sport even in public. On one occasion, the French ambassador was astonished to be admitted into the presence of, 'cardinals, whose only distinction was to imbibe much wine and vodka and to smoke tobacco'.

Almost certainly, the Most Drunken Council had its origins in Peter's own odd sense of humour and should be viewed in much the same way as his appointment of gouty cripples as footmen. Nevertheless, as recent research suggests, Peter's irreverent attitude may have been of vital importance in preparing him psychologically for the task of ecclesiastical reform. During his reign, Peter engaged in an ambitious reform of the church which overturned many established practices and which gave rise to the accusation that he was an atheist and Antichrist. Yet Peter himself was a Christian ruler, imbued with a strong sense of the faith: 'very zealous for religion and well versed in Holy Scripture'. Conceivably, the insulting behaviour of the Drunken Council helped both to fortify Peter's resolution and to harden his conscience, and so made indirectly possible his controversial programme of ecclesiastical reorganization.

* Peter's reform of the church took on a twofold character. The first and less controversial aspect of his work was to improve the quality of the clergy and redefine its goals. To this end, he issued a number of regulations which stressed the educational and moral role of the church rather than its ritualistic and contemplative one. His second and more radical task involved the reorganization of church government. In 1700, following the death of the patriarch, Peter 'temporarily' put the government of the church in the hands of the state chancery organization. Although the *prikaz* entrusted with the supervision of the church had no influence over doctrine, it possessed full control over all ecclesiastical revenues and appointments. The significance of this reorganization was noted by the English envoy:

1 The patriarchal power has been so dangerous that the present
Tsar on the death of the late patriarch, sequestrated the office,
committing the spiritual administration to the Archbishop of
Riazan and the management of the temporal affairs to a lay
5 commission, who have likewise the disposal of abbey lands and
revenues . . . which besides the annual advantage of 150 000
pounds sterling to the treasury, has yet broken their interest in
the country, where they have no freehold left.

This 'temporary' arrangement lasted until 1720 when Peter undertook a
second, decisive reform. Church government was now brought into line
with the new system of colleges, and an Ecclesiastical College was
established as a permanent replacement for the office of patriarch.
Although renamed the Most Holy Synod shortly afterwards, the new
body remained a branch of state government and its administration was
kept in the hands of secular officials. In the same year, Peter explained
his motives for reforming the church:

.1 The fatherland need not fear from an administrative council the
seditions and disorders that proceed from the personal rule of a
single church ruler. For the common folk do not perceive how
different is the ecclesiastical power from that of the Autocrat, but
5 dazzled by the greater honour and glory of the Supreme Pastor,
they think him a kind of second sovereign, equal or even greater
than the Autocrat himself, and imagine that the ecclesiastical
order is another and better state . . .

Ecclesiastical offices were never absorbed into the Table of Ranks.
Thus superficially at least the church was not subjected to the processes
of bureaucratization and militarization which affected other groups in
society. Nevertheless, the regulation of the church in the interests of
the state and the absorption of its government into the state administration remained the intended and most lasting consequence of Peter's
work of ecclesiastical reform.

7 The Legacy

Peter's reform of the church illustrates his passion for hierarchy and
regulation. Peter was firmly convinced that the proper organization and
ordering of government and society would make Muscovy a formidable
military power and would speed its transformation into a modern
European state. To this end, he cajoled his subjects with decrees and
enactments, bullied the peasantry into the army and drove the nobility
into his service. Any resistance or criticism was met with punishment
rather than with patient persuasion. Indeed, Peter's own son was to be
disinherited and put in jail for his opposition to the Tsar's coercive

regime. The severity and swiftness of punishment may explain the absence of any form of organized opposition to Peter's reforms.

The army was Peter's first love and remained his resort when other instruments of policy failed. In the army, orders were carried out unquestioningly and loyalty was unconditional. Its obedience and structure of command conveyed the illusion of efficiency. Whenever thus confronted with mismanagement or neglect, Peter believed military routines and the deployment of his officers would provide a speedy solution. In the 1720s the army was entrusted with the difficult task of collecting the soul tax; at the same time, lieutenants were appointed to investigate accusations of malpractice in the civil administration, even to the extent of interrogating senators; and a colonel was appointed head of the Most Holy Synod. By the end of Peter's reign, officers were attached to every government institution and the machinery of the state was fast becoming a branch of the military administration.

If military techniques provided a method, the example of the west provided the goal and inspiration. In his reform of government and society, Peter looked abroad for examples of how things ought to be done. The Swedish colleges and the Prussian *Rangordnung* were thus transplanted into Russia. Peter's vision of the future was similarly borrowed from abroad. Foreign architecture, dress and entertainments, were introduced to make Muscovy 'modern' in its appearance. By the close of Peter's reign, the dream of a new 'western' capital at St Petersburg had been made real. The wealthier landowners were summoned there and ordered to build stone houses on the basis of plans drawn up by the Tsar. Any refusal to do so was met with the confiscation of property. Thus even the finest and most enduring example of westernisation turned out like so much else in Peter's reign to have been built on coercion.

Despite the energy and ruthlessness which Peter put into the work of modernisation, the transformation which he effected was only partial. Much was undertaken in haste and, under the strain of war, in a haphazard fashion. Peter's reversals of policy in regard to the local administration suggest a lack of forward-planning, and the system he introduced barely outlasted his death. Likewise, the colleges were never put on a firm and lasting basis. By the mid-1720s, the functions of a number of colleges had already been broken up, and there were signs of a return to the older form of chancery government. Beneath the new names and titles, culled from western vocabulary, mismanagement and corruption abounded. Behind the strict hierarchy of ranks, personal and arbitrary rule by self-serving officials abounded. With the typical conceit of the despot, Peter imagined that he could force the Muscovite civil service to change its old ways and to embrace western standards of government.

Even in its effect on the broad mass of society, westernisation had only a limited impact. During Peter's reign, the peasants were

St Petersburg

The Winter Palace in St Petersburg

When I arrived [in St Petersburg], I was surprised to find instead of a regular city, as I expected, a heap of villages linked together, like some plantation in the West Indies. However, at present Petersburg may with reason be looked upon as a wonder of the world, considering its magnificent palaces, sixty odd thousand houses and the short time that was employed in the building of it.

F. C. Weber, *The Present State of Russia* (London, 1722)

There reigns in this capital a kind of bastard architecture, which partakes of the Italian, the French and the Dutch: this last is, however, the most prevalent . . . The Tsar obliged the Boyars and Grandees of the Empire to leave Moscow, in the neighbourhood of which their estates were, and to settle where the court removed to. The palaces of most of them are upon the banks of the Neva, and it is easy to see that they were built out of obedience rather than choice. Their walls are all cracked, quite out of perpendicular, and ready to fall. It has been wittily enough said, that ruins make themselves in other places, but that they were built at Petersburg.

Count Francesco Algarotti, *Letters to Lord Hervey* (London, 1769) dragooned and oppressed even more than before, for they were now the chattels of the state as well as the property of their masters. Their service on the land was expanded to include service in the army or in the labour battalions which built St Petersburg. But for all this, they remained ignorant of western ideas and culture. The bewigged, perfumed noblemen, now drawn from their country estates to serve in the Ranks, became increasingly remote from their bearded counterparts. The deep cleavage between noble and peasant, which distinguishes Russian history down to this century, has its roots in Peter's failure to complete the process of westernisation. Another revolution would be needed to bridge the great gulf his labour of reform had dug across Russian society.

Making notes on 'Peter the Great and Russia'

This chapter is primarily concerned with Peter's work of domestic reform and with the modernisation and westernisation of Muscovite government and society. In reading this chapter you should pay special attention to Peter's motives and goals, and to the extent to which his achievements proved either superficial or impermanent. The following headings and questions should help you to make notes:

1. Interpreting Peter the Great
2. Westernisation before Peter
2.1. Previous contacts and attitudes
2.2. Seventeenth-century doubts and developments
3. The 'Great Embassy' to the west
3.1. Early years and the Princess Sophie
3.2. Azov
3.3. The 'Great Embassy'. What does the story of the 'Great Embassy' reveal about Peter's attitude towards the west and about the attitudes of Europeans towards Muscovy?
4. The impact of war
4.1. Initial reforms and the outbreak of war
4.2. Military expansion
4.3. Recruitment
4.4. Education
4.5. Industry
How did the war with Sweden influence the pattern and pace of modernisation in Muscovy?
5. Finance and administration
5.1. The 'artery of war' and the soul tax
5.2. Administrative reform: chanceries, governments, colleges and Senate
5.3. The Table of Ranks

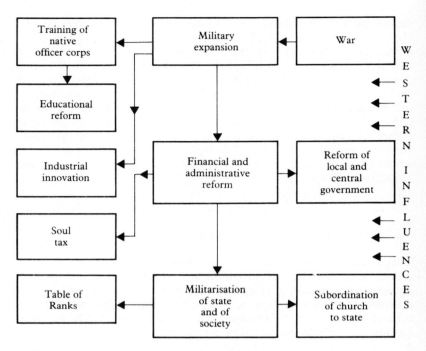

The domestic reforms of Peter the Great

To what extent had Peter made Muscovite society 'geared for war' by the end of his reign?
6.   The church
6.1. The prestige and reputation of the orthodox church
6.2. The Most Drunken Council
6.3. Reform and subordination
7.   The legacy. What evidence is contained in this section to suggest that Peter's work of reform was superficial and incomplete by the time of his death?

Source-based questions on 'Peter the Great and Russia'

1 Western Impressions
Read the descriptions of Peter the Great given by the imperial ambassador and by the Bishop of Salisbury on page 88, and the English ambassador's account on page 89 of the behaviour of the

Muscovite envoys in Adrianople. Answer the following questions:

a) What do the imperial and the English ambassadors' accounts tell us about western attitudes towards Peter the Great and to his early work of reform?

b) In what respects do the imperial ambassador and the Bishop of Salisbury agree in their estimate of Peter. In what ways do their opinions differ?

c) For what reasons did Peter embark on his 'Great Embassy' to the west? What were the consequences for Muscovy of his tour in Europe?

2 Modernisation and Reform

Read the accounts given of the chanceries and colleges on page 94 and of the building of St Petersburg on page 98. Look also at the pictures given on these pages of the college buildings and of the Winter Palace in St Petersburg. Answer the following questions:

a) What, according to Peterson, were the principal limitations of the older system of chancery administration? To what extent does the extract from a contemporary memorandum support Peterson's opinion of the defects inherent in the old system?

b) What do the accounts of the Swedish ambassador and of Count Algarotti reveal about the aptitude and interest of Peter's subjects in his work of modernisation and reform?

c) To what extent does the construction and architecture of the Winter Palace and of the Colleges coincide with the opinions given of St Petersburg by Weber and Algarotti?

d) In what areas of reform and improvement, other than architecture and administration, did Peter the Great draw inspiration from western examples?

3 The Church

Read the account of the patriarch's authority given by the German scholar on page 93; the description of the Most Drunken Council on pages 95 to 96; the English envoy's explanation on page 96; and Peter's own account of his motives on page 96. Answer the following questions:

a) What was the Most Drunken Council? Might its buffoonery, as described here, have served any deeper purpose?

b) In what ways might the prestige and influence of the patriarch, as described by the German scholar, have posed a threat to the Tsar's own authority?

c) To what extent do the English envoy's account and Peter's own explanation indicate that the office of patriarch was indeed considered at this time to present a political threat?

d) What other motives, hinted at by the English envoy, may explain Peter's interest in taking over the administration of the church?

CHAPTER 6

Peter the Great, Poland and the Ukraine

1 The Great Northern War

During the first decades of the eighteenth century, Muscovy burst upon the European stage, effecting a revolution in diplomatic relations and establishing its mastery of the Baltic region. Under Peter's direction, Muscovy became (and has remained ever since) one of Europe's great powers; previously it had counted for little in international affairs. Discussing this transformation, the French ambassador to St Petersburg remarked, 'Russia, formerly scarcely known by name, has today become the object of the attention of most of the European powers, who seek its friendship either by fear of seeing it take the side opposed to them or through the advantage which they hope for from its alliance'. In token of the great alteration in his country's international reputation, Peter announced in 1721 that he should henceforward be referred to in diplomatic correspondence no longer as Tsar of Muscovy but instead as Emperor or *Imperator* of Russia. By assuming this new title, Peter emphasised both his leading place among the crowned heads of Europe and how greatly his country had been transformed from the remote Muscovy of his predecessors.

* Of course, Peter's Russia did not make its debut as a great power unannounced. From the late fifteenth century onwards, Muscovy had been steadily making closer diplomatic and political contact with the rest of Europe. During Ivan III's reign, Muscovite envoys had presented themselves in Germany in the hope of winning imperial support against the Lithuanians. Under Ivan IV relations were established with distant England. In the next century, Michael Romanov actively supported the Protestant side in the Thirty Years' War, providing Denmark and Sweden with cheap grain and fodder. By the early 1630s the anti-Habsburg diplomatic axis which stretched across Europe linking Paris to Stockholm and to Transylvania had been extended eastwards to include Moscow.

Despite these contacts, Muscovy continued throughout the seventeenth century to merit little attention from western statesmen. Her envoys were therefore not included in the discussions which ended the Thirty Years' War; nor was Muscovy invited to the share-out of lands which accompanied the conclusion of the Scanian War (1674–79) and the temporary eclipse of Sweden as a Baltic power. Even as late as 1701, Peter's envoy in Vienna summed up the scornful attitude of foreign diplomats towards Muscovy with the sad words, 'They only laugh at us'.

At the start of his reign, Peter directed most of his warlike energies in a bid to secure an outlet to the Black Sea. Peter hoped to follow up his capture of Azov by an assault on the Turkish-held Straits of Kerch. For this, however, he needed the support of the other European powers. Peter's failure at the time of his 'Great Embassy' to win the international help he needed, only confirmed the lack of regard with which his country was held in the courts of Europe. As Peter put it, 'In my lifetime I shall never forget what they [the European statesmen] have done to me; I feel it, and am come off with empty pockets'.

* For all the failure attending the 'Great Embassy', one substantial offer of alliance was received. In August 1698, Peter met the King of Poland, Augustus II, and in a prolonged drinking-bout the two monarchs agreed to a military partnership against the King of Sweden. At this time, Sweden was apparently in decline. After the Scanian War, the country had lost a large part of its Baltic empire and in Livonia a rebellion of the local nobility against Swedish rule had recently broken out. The new King of Sweden, Charles XII, was only 17 years old and was reckoned too inexperienced and too harried at home by his parliament to be much of a match. Over the next months, Augustus and Peter added Brandenburg–Prussia and Denmark to their intrigues and they planned together the partition of the Swedish Empire. Muscovy would receive Ingria and Karelia; Augustus would obtain Livonia and Estonia; and their allies would share out the remaining Swedish territories on the German coast. Unfortunately for the conspirators, they had severely underestimated both the young King and the resources still available to their Swedish prey.

Peter's motives for making war on Sweden were threefold. Firstly, as in his previous campaign against the Turks, he was simply eager for a fight. Thus he allowed himself to be thrown into the fray 'like a skittle in a game of bowls', embarking on a war for which he was ill prepared. Secondly, the Swedish territories of Karelia and Ingria were ancient Russian lands, only lost recently in the 'Time of Troubles'. Thirdly, if Muscovy was to become a European power, it needed access to the sea. The Black Sea was blocked by the Straits of Kerch; Archangel was remote and icebound. The Baltic Sea, however, could serve as an avenue to Holland and England, the countries Peter had visited on his recent tour. For motives, therefore, not dissimilar to those which had once prompted Ivan IV to make war in the Baltic, Peter took Muscovy into conflict with Sweden.

* In August 1700, Peter commenced hostilities. While the Polish army advanced on Riga, he invested Narva. Within a few months, however, the armies of the coalition were in sorry retreat. Denmark was rapidly forced out of the war by an attack on Copenhagen and Brandenburg–Prussia, witnessing this defeat, refused to join in the war.

Thereafter, Charles XII set about driving his enemies from the territories they had overrun. In November 1700, Peter's army was smashed at the Battle of Narva.

Had Charles so chosen, he might have advanced deep into Muscovy and, as one of his supporters urged, 'reigned in Moscow as far as the River Amur [the border with China]'. Instead, however, Charles relieved Riga and broke into the Polish Commonwealth. Despite his rapid victory over the Polish forces, Charles obtained no greater mastery of the Commonwealth's affairs than its elected monarchs. For five long years, his energies were dissipated in various unsuccessful attempts to establish Swedish rule in Poland's political quagmire.

Charles XII's involvement in Poland gave Peter both a vital breathing-space in which to build his armies and the opportunity to nibble away in the Baltic. In 1702–3, Peter overran the Swedish forts on the Gulf of Finland. On the site of one of these, he built the citadel which over the next few years was to be transformed into the city of St Petersburg. Shortly afterwards, Peter began edging into Estonia and Livonia. But these were fragile successes, obtained only by reason of Sweden's temporary involvement elsewhere. Once divested of the problems of Polish politics, Sweden would be able to make good its losses and recover the initiative in the east.

2 Augustus II

Peter's partner in the Great Northern War was Augustus II, who had been elected King of the Commonwealth in 1697. Augustus II possessed many remarkable qualities. He had had a chequered youth, spent variously as a monk and a matador, and even in middle age exhibited enormous strength. Universally known as 'Augustus the Strong', he could break horseshoes in his hands and consume vast quantities of alcohol while still remaining upright. 'Half bull, half cock', as one of his subjects described him, he left some 300 authenticated bastards as evidence of his prodigious stamina.

In political affairs Augustus displayed rather less talent than in his private life. At the time of his election, he was also Duke of Saxony and his German homeland always counted for more in his designs than did his adopted one. Therefore, when Augustus joined Peter in attacking Sweden, he aimed to make Livonia a part of Saxony rather than of Poland. As it turned out, Augustus failed to obtain Livonia and, by taking on Sweden, lost the crown of Poland as well. The eventual recovery of his fortunes owed much to Peter the Great's intervention on his behalf and his reign left the Commonwealth a virtual satellite of its more powerful neighbour.

Augustus's initial failure to capture Riga was followed by a series of dismal defeats. Courland was occupied by the Swedes and shortly afterwards Vilna, Warsaw and Cracow were taken by Charles XII. In two great battles, the Swedes routed the Polish army which the *Seym* had hastily gathered against them. Faced with overwhelming Swedish superiority on the field, Lithuania's leading family, the Sapiehas, put the duchy under Swedish protection and announced its secession from the Commonwealth. To add to Augustus's misery, Charles XII gathered together those of the Polish *szlachta* willing to follow the Sapiehas' example. In 1704, the 'Confederation of Warsaw', as this group of disaffected noblemen entitled their organization, elected one of their number, Stanislas Leszczynski, as King. Two years later, Charles took the decisive step of invading Saxony, whither Augustus had fled. Having occupied Dresden, Charles forced the humiliated King to abdicate the Polish throne in favour of Stanislas I.

3 Mazeppa

According to the terms of the Truce of Andrusovo (1667), the Ukraine was divided between Poland and Muscovy along the line of the River Dnieper. However, the partition of the Ukraine into a 'west bank' and an 'east bank', brought no relief to its troubled inhabitants. The tide of war, enserfment and political subjection continued to spill over the region, prompting in its train a series of uprisings and rebellions. The most serious of these occurred during the first years of the Great Northern War under the leadership of the Cossack Hetman, Ivan Mazeppa. By making common cause with the Swedes, Mazeppa was able to lend his rebellion an international significance far greater than its essentially local character would otherwise have allowed.

The Hetman Mazeppa, who had ruled the eastern part of the Ukraine as a vassal of the Tsar since 1687, was a representative of the wealthier element of Cossacks. Over the preceding decades an élite of Cossacks had established itself as a kind of native Ukrainian nobility and hereditary officer-corps. In both the Polish and Muscovite parts of the Ukraine, the Cossack *shliakta* or *starshina* (the first of these terms means 'nobility', the second 'staff-officer'; their synonymity indicates the continuing association among the Cossacks of social prestige and military leadership) had amassed estates and serf-villages of their own and had gradually acquired a monopoly of power in the region. For these reasons, Mazeppa and his *starshina* saw nothing to be gained from disloyalty to Moscow. Instead, they helped suppress all popular insurrections and joined the Tsar in his wars against the Turks and the Swedes.

During the first years of the eighteenth century, a Cossack revolt in west-bank Ukraine had gathered sufficient strength as to undermine the Polish contribution to the Great Northern War. In 1704, therefore, Peter instructed Mazeppa to cross the Dnieper and bring his Cossack compatriots to heel. Mazeppa proceeded to overrun west-bank

Ukraine, where he took over the government and proclaimed himself 'Hetman of All Ukraine'.

Peter had no intention of allowing his vassal to annex the Polish Ukraine and he ordered Mazeppa to return the region he had overrun. Plainly though, by this stage the Hetman had designs of his own. In 1707, Mazeppa entered into negotiations with the pro-Swedish King of Poland, Stanislas Leszczynski, aimed at establishing a united Ukrainian state, semi-independent under the Polish crown. Mazeppa's intrigues apparently bore fruit when Leszczynski offered him a document 'which contained guarantees for the Ukraine of the same liberties that the Polish crownlands and the Lithuanian duchy enjoy'.

* Throughout his secret negotiations with King Stanislas, Mazeppa maintained a show of loyalty to Peter. However, in 1708 he was forced to reveal his hand. Charles XII had recently launched a massive invasion of Muscovy. His armies bore eastwards, driving Peter out of the Baltic provinces (only St Petersburg remained), and pushing across White Russia. But a scorched earth policy followed by a bitterly cold winter slowed the Swedish advance and obliged Charles to reconsider his strategy. Instead of maintaining the thrust towards Smolensk and Muscovy, Charles wheeled his army southwards into the warmer and more fertile Ukraine. In the late autumn of 1708 the Swedish troops broke out of the Severian forest on to the grassland of the northern steppes and Charles demanded Mazeppa's immediate help against the pursuing Muscovite forces. After only a little delay, the Hetman threw off his mask of loyalty and joined the Swedes.

At a gathering of the Cossack *starshina*, Mazeppa justified his treason by reference to the brutalities of Muscovite rule and the hope which he put in his Swedish ally. As he explained:

1 The only solution for us is to rely on the compassion of the Swedish King. He has promised to respect our rights and liberties and to protect them from all those who would threaten them. Brothers! Our time has come. Let us use the opportunity to
5 avenge ourselves on the Muscovites for their longstanding oppression, for all the injustices and cruelties they have inflicted. Let us preserve for the future our liberty and our Cossack rights from their incursions.

Peter railed against 'the deeds of the new Judas, Mazeppa, who after 21 years of loyalty to me and with one foot already in the grave, has turned traitor and betrayer of his own people'. But he quickly recovered from his fury. Within a week a Muscovite detachment had seized Mazeppa's capital at Baturin and Peter was working hard to sow divisions in the Cossack ranks. In his propaganda, the Tsar exploited the distrust with which the rank-and-file held the *starshina*. He denounced the Hetman's greed and the heavy taxes he had laid on the population solely 'to augment his own riches'. Contesting Mazeppa's claim that his revolt was aimed at the liberation of the Ukraine, Peter described the Hetman as seeking 'to return the Ukraine to Polish slavery'. The efficacy of Peter's publicity was speedily felt. Within a few weeks, Mazeppa's forces had dwindled to little more than 1500 men, and the Tsar had gathered sufficient support to have the Cossack council depose the Hetman.

* Not all, however, was lost to Mazeppa. In April 1709 he scored a

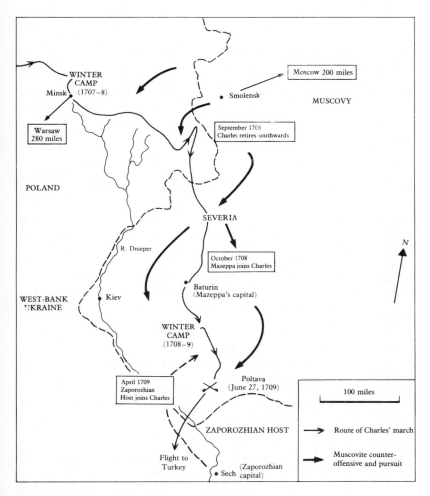

Charles XII's invasion of Muscovy, 1708–9

major victory when the Zaporozhian Host voted to support him against the Tsar. The self-governing Cossack community furnished Mazeppa and his Swedish ally with at least 6000 troops. As a first step, the Host's army put to flight three of the regiments sent against it. Much concerned, the Muscovite commander in the region reported to Peter that the tide of war was turning in the enemy's favour and that, 'a great conflagration is developing here and it must be put out before it is too late'.

Peter's response was determined and bold. In May 1709 a detachment of his army captured and razed the Zaporozhian capital, which had been left inadequately garrisoned. Thereafter, some 40 000 Muscovite troops descended upon the much smaller Swedish and Cossack army which was then camped outside the town of Poltava. Within a few hours, the superior Muscovite forces had taken the field and had routed their enemy. Charles and Mazeppa did not halt their flight until they had reached the relative safety of the Ottoman Empire. Later that year, Mazeppa died: a fugitive guarded by Swedish troops from the wrath of his Cossack followers. It was six years before Charles XII was able to escape his virtual captivity and return home to Sweden.

4 The Silent *Seym*

The Battle of Poltava (1709) marked the conclusion of the Ukrainian phase of the Great Northern War, and ushered in a succession of Muscovite victories. With the Swedish King now in virtual captivity in Turkish Moldavia and his army and Cossack allies dispersed after their recent defeat, Peter's new offensive in the Baltic met little resistance. In the same year as Poltava, Estonia, Ingria and Livonia fell to the Muscovite army, and Riga, Reval and Narva were stormed. With the Baltic coastline secure, Peter invaded Poland, where he routed Leszczyski and the pro-Swedish Confederation of Warsaw. In 1710 Augustus and the Saxon monarchy was restored in the baggage train of the Muscovite army.

Once returned to Poland, Augustus sought to impose his will on the *Seym* and *szlachta*. With the help of his Saxon guardsmen he endeavoured to curb the liberties of his subjects, which he believed partly responsible for his earlier humiliations. Augustus's programme of reform, modest though it was, immediately provoked the *szlachta*'s suspicion that he was about to erect a 'foreign absolutism'. In 1715 the Polish nobility and *Seym* joined together in the Confederation of Tarnogrod with the aim of expelling Augustus and his Saxon entourage. Civil war erupted once more in Poland.

Peter was by now utterly fed up with the lamentable condition of his neighbour and spoke disparagingly of the 'Polish anarchy'. Until the Commonwealth was brought to order, its reliability as an ally could never be assured. Moreover, as Charles XII had shown, Poland's weakness and internal divisions made it an easy target for foreign intrigue and a potential springboard for an attack on Muscovy itself. Hitherto, Peter had endeavoured to influence Polish affairs by giving support to its monarch. The Confederation of Tarnogrod spelled the failure of this policy and obliged him to embark on a more direct involvement.

In 1716 Peter offered to arbitrate in the dispute between Augustus and the Confederation. His solution was to have both sides give up their means of harming each other. Augustus thus promised to withdraw his Saxon troops and the *Seym* promised to limit the Polish army to 12 000 men. Such a pitifully small force left Poland at the mercy of the Tsar's own forces and prepared the way for the 'Silent *Seym*' of 1717.

The year after he had settled the quarrel between Augustus and his subjects, Peter requested that the *Seym* recognise the agreement he had negotiated. The building in which the *Seym* met was surrounded by 18 000 Muscovite troops whose presence ensured that the debate was conducted with unusual haste. In less than a day, the deputies agreed not only to the permanent reduction of the Polish army but also to Muscovy acting as guarantor of the constitution. The second condition of the agreement allowed Peter to intervene at will in the Commonwealth's affairs; the former removed any possibility of resisting him by force. As a sign of 'good faith' Peter agreed to keep some of his regiments on Polish soil. Not one voice was raised in the *Seym* against these terms; they were heard and accepted in silence. For more than 250 years, the 'friendly protection' offered to Poland by Russia has remained a part of east European politics. Such is a testimony both to the farsightedness of Peter's policy and to the continuing interest of his successors in 'propagating tyranny under the pretext of correcting anarchy' (De Custine).

5 The Turk of the North

The victory of Poltava did not by any means put an end to the dangerous influence of Peter's Swedish rival. Even in what he called his 'sluggard's days in Turkey', Charles worked hard to undermine the Tsar's military achievement by encouraging the Sultan to go to war on his behalf. Eventually, in 1711 Charles's persuasion prevailed and the Turks opened hostilities against Muscovy. In the campaign which followed, Peter was worsted and was subsequently forced to surrender the town of Azov, which his armies had captured at the start of his reign. Peter regretted the loss, but fortified himself with the knowledge that Azov was of only secondary importance. As he wrote, 'Although it is not without grief that we are deprived of those places where so much labour and money have been expended, yet I hope that by this very deprivation we shall greatly strengthen ourselves on the other side [the Baltic], which is of incomparably greater gain to us'.

* As the Swedish Empire in the Baltic crumbled, Peter increasingly found himself the object of European diplomatic attention. Muscovy had now replaced Sweden as the leading state in northern Europe and had by the victory at Poltava effected a transformation in the regional balance of power. As one German observer wrote, 'You can imagine how the great revolution in the north has astounded many people. It is commonly being said that the Tsar will be formidable to the whole of Europe, that he will be as though a "Turk of the North".' In England, the Earl of Godolphin wrote in more alarmed fashion to the Duke of Marlborough, 'Those northern provinces, which the King of Sweden has kept so long in awe, will now be very troublesome if timely measures be not concerted . . . to hinder any possible novelties in those parts.'

International concern at the growth of Russian power in the Baltic mounted with each of Peter's victories. In 1714 his army overran Finland and his navy defeated the Swedish fleet at the Battle of Gangut. The return of Charles XII to Stockholm the next year brought little relief to the hard-pressed Swedes and for a short time a Muscovite army established itself on the mainland, ravaging the area around the capital. However, it was less the defeat of the Swedes as the extension of Muscovite power into Germany and western Europe which caused the greatest alarm. In 1716 Peter amassed a 30000-strong army which he shipped to Copenhagen in readiness for an invasion of southern Sweden. Although leave of passage had been agreed by the King of Denmark, the magnitude of Peter's army posed a major threat to Danish independence. In the same year, Peter marched a second army into Mecklenburg, in north Germany, with the purpose of attacking the Swedish-held town of Wismar. These two actions spelled the effective transformation of the Baltic Sea into a 'Russian lake', its coastline from Livonia to Jutland becoming a barracks for Peter's regiments.

* During 1719–20 considerable international pressure was put on Peter to withdraw his forces eastwards and to break off the war with Sweden. The principal power behind the gathering European coalition, which included Prussia, Austria and France, was Great Britain. Both George I and his ministers feared in particular the implications for commerce of Muscovy obtaining a monopoly of influence in the Baltic, a region on which Britain depended for naval supplies and mastage (in effect, tall pine trees). In order to bring Peter to diplomatic sense, a British fleet was despatched to patrol the Livonian coast.

Peter bowed to the inevitability of peace. In 1721 at the Peace of Nystad, Muscovy and Sweden came to terms. Livonia, Estonia, Ingria and Karelia, and thus the entire Baltic coastline from Vyborg to Riga, were given over to Russia. In return, Peter ceded Finland and promised to allow the Swedish purchase of grain in his ports. On the map of Europe, the territories won by Peter at Nystad appear too insignificant to have been worth 20 years of continuous warfare. However, the

Russia and eastern Europe during the reign of Peter the Great

implications of Nystad both for the international balance of power and for Russian access to the rest of Europe were unmistakable. As the cannons roared in St Petersburg to salute the treaty, Peter delivered the following words of congratulation and admonition to his subjects:

1 By our deeds in war we have emerged from darkness into the light of the world, and those whom we did not know in the light now respect us. I wish our entire nation to recognise the direct hand of God in our favour during the last war and in the conclusion of this
5 peace. It becomes us to thank God with all our might, but while hoping for peace, we must not grow weaker in military matters, so as not to have the fate of the Greek [Byzantine] monarchy. We must make efforts for the general good and profit which may God grant us at home and abroad and from which the nation will
10 receive advantage.

6 Russia as a European Power

The cause of Peter's death befitted his impetuosity and energy. In the winter of 1724, while travelling near St Petersburg, he spotted a ship driven aground by bad weather. Immediately, he leapt into the water and worked throughout the night to save the lives of 20 of the sailors. Peter never recovered from the fever he contracted during the rescue. He died on 28th January 1725, at the relatively young age of 52. At Peter's funeral, the Archbishop of Novgorod pronounced a verdict on his reign:

1 He was your Samson, O Russia! He found you with little strength and left you . . . strong as a rock, as a diamond . . . Russia, he was your first Japhet! He carried out an enterprise hitherto unheard of in Russia – the building and launching of ships, of a fleet new
5 born but yielding in nothing to old-established ones . . . He was your Moses, O Russia! Are not his laws like the strong visor of justice and the unbreakable chains repressing crime? O Russia! He was your Solomon, receiving from the Lord abundance of wisdom and reason. Do we not have sufficient proof in the new
10 intellectual disciplines which he introduced and in his efforts to point out and communicate to many of his subjects a great variety of knowledge, inventions and techniques before unknown to us? And what of the ranks and titles, the civil laws, the well-chosen regulations regarding social life, the welcome new customs and
15 rules of conduct, the improvements introduced into our external appearance, so that we look at ourselves and are astonished to see our fatherland visibly changed and become incomparably super-ior to what it was before? He was your David and your Constan-

tine, O Russian Church! Drawn from the paths of ignorance, our
20 hearts give forth a sigh of relief.

With rather less hyperbole, a young naval officer wrote, 'This monarch
has brought our country to a level with others. He taught us to
recognise that we are a people. In brief, everything that we look upon in
Russia has its origins in him and everything which is done in the future
will be determined from this source.'
 * If we put aside the funeral rhetoric and examine Peter's reign with
the benefit of hindsight, it is clear that Peter brought Russia to a
European 'level' more by way of his accomplishments in foreign affairs
than by way of his internal, domestic reforms. As we have seen, Peter's
transformation of Russian government and society proceeded unevenly
and its impact largely missed the broad mass of the population.
Constrastingly, Peter's reign put Muscovy's relations with the rest of
Europe on a completely new footing and he achieved a total transformation in international power-politics. Although the succinct phrase,
'Russia is a European power' was penned by Catherine the Great
(1762–96), it may equally well apply to the Russia of Peter the Great.
 A telling indication of the new esteem with which Peter's Russia was
held in Europe is dynastic intermarriage. Poor old Ivan IV had been
unable to win the hand of even the second-rate English heiress, Lady
Mary Hastings, and his seventeenth-century successors had fared no
better on the European marriage-market. During Peter's reign, however, the Russian ruling family began to be accepted as a source of
respectable and worthy spouses. Certainly, little glamour was attached
to these marriages, contracted invariably between 'ungainly Russian
princesses and obscure German princelets'. Nevertheless, Peter's own
proposal, made at the end of his reign, to marry his daughter to a
French Bourbon prince was considered seriously in Versailles. Louis
XV's rejection of the match originated not from sentiments of distaste
or disdain but from the implications which a Russian marriage held for
his foreign policy.
 Dynastic marriages were negotiated by diplomats and by the 1720s
Russia had established ambassadorial contact with all the leading
European courts. With more than 20 foreign missions, Russia was
continuously involved in all the principal discussions affecting relations
between the powers. As one of Peter's advisers reported, 'Today the
Russians have so many ministers and emissaries at foreign courts that
they are ignorant of nothing that happens there'.
 * Where her diplomats trod, Russia's armies soon followed. In the
century after Peter's death, Russia became increasingly enmeshed in
European conflicts. During the Seven Years War (1756–63), Russia
fought on the side of the Habsburgs and France against Great Britain
and Prussia. In 1760 her forces were in Berlin. In the 1770s the Russian
navy sailed the Mediterranean in pursuit of the Turks. Half a century

later, at the end of the Napoleonic Wars, a Russian garrison was installed in Paris. Such was the legacy of the Great Northern War, during the course of which Russia had toppled its Swedish neighbour, established its hegemony in the Baltic, and won its credentials as a European power. It is a legacy with which the states of Europe must reckon even today.

7 Russia, Poland and the Ukraine

It would of course be wrong to attribute Russia's status as a European power solely to the work of Peter the Great. Peter built on the accomplishments of his predecessors as surely as he laid a foundation of his own for the future. For this reason, his achievements should be viewed neither in isolation nor as a starting-point of Russian expansion. They were instead all part of a longer process of territorial acquisition the effects of which continue to be felt even today and the origins of which can ultimately be traced back to the middle ages.

Muscovy had first broken out of its obscure forest fastness and had embarked on a programme of imperial conquest under its late medieval rulers. Ivan III had begun the drive towards hegemony over the broad belt of land lying between the Baltic and Black Seas. Lithuanians, Tatars and petty princelings had been the earliest foes of the Tsars. However, the rulers of Moscow had soon come into conflict with the Poles and with the Cossacks of the Ukraine. Throughout the sixteenth and seventeenth centuries, Muscovy had been engaged in a prolonged struggle with both these nations; it was into this three-cornered contest that the Swedes had descended. The defeat of Charles XII by Peter the Great made possible Russian mastery of the entire eastern part of the European Plain and thus of a substantial part of the east European mainland.

a) Poland

The 80 years following the Silent *Seym* are among the most tragic and inglorious in Polish history. On the basis of the agreement made between Peter and the *Seym* in 1717 the Russian rulers regularly interfered in Polish affairs to preserve the constitution and thus the chief source of the Commonwealth's weakness. Polish deputies in Russian pay constantly vetoed all proposals made in the *Seym* which were deemed harmful to Poland's neighbour. At election time, Russian cash and regiments ensured that the *szlachta* played to the right tune and swallowed its pride. On the death of Augustus II, his son, Augustus III, succeeded with the help of Russian bayonets. Upon his death in 1763, the Empress Catherine the Great of Russia arranged for the election of her former lover to the throne. On this occasion, the *szlachta* met on a field surrounded by Russian troops. As the victor himself noted, his was the least difficult election in all the Commonwealth's history.

By this time, the collapse of the Commonwealth was complete. The *Seym* ceased to conduct any business; the small army stayed in its barracks; and the economy was reduced to ruins. Foreign troops marched unimpeded across Polish soil, making the country little more than a 'wayside inn for armies'. Only in the palaces and on the great estates of the magnates was any sense of order obtained or of cultural achievement manifested.

The end came with the partitions of 1773, 1793, and 1795. In three stages, Poland's neighbours dismembered the Commonwealth, consuming it like an artichoke, leaf by leaf (as Frederick the Great graphically put it). In the distribution of the spoils, Prussia received Warsaw and Austria Cracow, but it was Russia which obtained the lion's share: roughly 65 per cent of the Commonwealth's landmass and 70 per cent of its population. This was the first time a European state had been so mercilessly and completely carved up. The opinion in the courts of Europe was that somehow Poland had deserved her fate by reason of her disabling constitution. The fact that all reform of the constitution had been blocked by the Russian Tsars and army was conveniently overlooked.

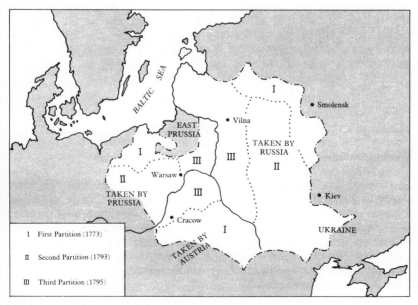

The partitions of Poland

b) The Ukraine

The Russian subjugation of the Ukraine proceeded simultaneously with its subjugation of the Commonwealth. Indeed, the fate of the two regions was joined together since at the time of the Second Partition (1793), the greater part of West Ukraine was annexed by Russia.

After Mazeppa's defeat in 1709 the office of Hetman on the east bank of the Dnieper was alternately abolished and resurrected under puppet governments. Eventually in 1764 Catherine the Great determined 'to destroy the very name of Hetman and not merely appoint a weakling to the office', and she accordingly transferred the entire administration of the Ukraine to Moscow. During her reign, what little autonomy remained to the Zaporozhian Host was likewise removed and the last of the Host's Hetmans was exiled to the White Sea. Following the dismantling of the old Ukrainian administration, those of the better-off Cossacks remaining in the region were absorbed within the ranks of the Russian nobility. Although their status lacked clear definition, they were effectively transformed into a pliant service-class of landowners. Their humbler counterparts were meanwhile reduced to the condition of serfs or else recruited into the army as cavalrymen.

In the western part of the Ukraine, organized opposition to 'polonisation' and to 'landlordism' gradually petered out. The brief flurries of popular insurrection swiftly degenerated into brigandage and indiscriminate looting. Thus the unification of the Ukraine under Russian rule in 1793 occurred at a time when the region had already been deprived not only of its vestiges of self-government but also of its spirit of resistance. Only in the nineteenth century, under the influence of romanticism and the new mood of national revival, would the Ukraine awaken to a sense of its own statehood and find in its Cossacks a powerful symbol of its ancient struggle for independence.

Making notes on 'Peter the Great, Poland and the Ukraine'

In reading this chapter you should concentrate in particular on how Peter's victory in the Great Northern War allowed him to establish Russian supremacy in the Baltic region and to subjugate both Poland and the Ukraine. Importantly also, you should realise that the Great Northern War made Russia a European power and transformed its reputation in the eyes of foreign contemporaries. The following headings and questions should help you to make notes:
1.   The Great Northern War
1.1. Russia's reputation by the end of Peter's reign
1.2. Antecedents and attitudes

1.3. The Great Northern War: aims and allies

1.4. Narva: Peter defeated and spared

What does the suddenness of Peter's attack on Sweden and the rapidity of his defeat tell us about his qualities as a ruler and commander?

2.   Augustus II. To which did Augustus's humiliation owe more: the Swedish invasion or his subjects' rebellion? What do Augustus's experiences tell us about the weaknesses of the Commonwealth?

3.   Mazeppa

3.1. The Ukraine under Mazeppa

3.2. Charles XII and Mazeppa

3.3. The Zaporozhian Host

Why after years of loyalty to Peter did Mazeppa throw in his lot with the Swedes?

4.   The Silent *Seym*. Why should the *Seym* have agreed to the conditions laid down by Peter in 1717?

5.   The Turk of the North

5.1. The loss of Azov

5.2. International concern

5.3. The Peace of Nystad

Why were the statemen of western Europe so concerned by the spread of Russian influence in the Baltic region?

6.   Russia as a European Power

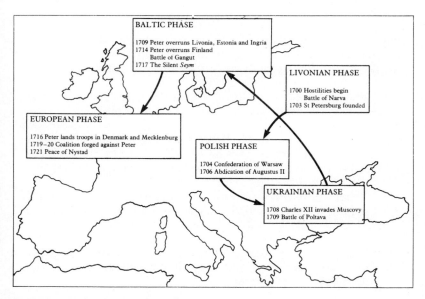

Phases of the Great Northern War

Answering essay questions on 'Peter the Great, Poland and the Ukraine'

Questions on Peter the Great at A-level often involve consideration of the entirety of his reign and embrace both his foreign and his domestic policies:

1. 'What did Peter the Great do for Russia?'

2. 'Assess the impact of Peter the Great on the development of Russia.'

Alternatively, questions will identify one particular area for analysis, usually Peter's participation in the Great Northern War, his reform of government, or the impact of westernisation on Russian society:

3. 'What did Peter hope to achieve in the Great Northern War and how successful was he in obtaining his aims?'

4. '"Russia's success in the Baltic between 1700 and 1721 owed more to the errors of Charles XII than to the military achievements of Peter the Great." Do you agree?'

5. '"Peter the Great's reforms, important though they were, brought no fundamental change to Russian government." Discuss.'

6. '"He worked on Russia like nitric acid on iron." To what extent was Russian society only superficially affected by the reforms of Peter the Great?'

In tackling the first two questions, you should avoid giving a simple catalogue of Peter's achievements. This is particularly the case with the 'What did Peter do?' question which invites the incautious response, 'He did a lot as I will now tell you in great detail'. Set your own limits to each question in the opening paragraph to your essay and outline the argument and approach you will follow in the main body of your work. This, of course, requires you to know in advance what you will write and makes careful planning particularly important. You might therefore start: *Peter accomplished much for Russia and his work of reform affected government, society and the church. In European affairs, he made his country a first-rate power. However, in domestic matters the impact of his reign proved limited, and in his foreign policy he built on the achievements of his predecessors. Thus he may be presumed to have accomplished less than a superficial examination of his work tends to suggest.* Let us suppose that you have written this. A structure for your essay has now been made apparent and a basic paragraph plan has emerged: government, society, the church, foreign affairs, limitations of domestic reform, the work of Peter's predecessors. What would you now include in each of the individual paragraphs? What information would you use to back up the points you have made? How would you conclude your essay?

In approaching the third question a basic structure for your essay is actually given in the title:

What were Peter's aims in the Great Northern War?
Did he achieve his aims?

You may choose therefore to divide your essay in half, explaining aims and achievements in separate sections. In your conclusion you could also indicate the extent to which Peter may have overfulfilled his ambitions and obtained more than he had originally planned. What evidence would you use to support such a point of view?

Although more complex in its composition, the fourth question contains like the third the structure of your answer within its title. What were:

the Russian successes in the Baltic
the errors of Charles XII
the military achievements of Peter the Great?

And:

which of the last two better explains the first?

Questions on Peter's reform of government and society are invariably concerned with the issue of their superficiality and originality. Therefore, it is worthwhile considering this matter in some detail before you actually sit the exam. Otherwise, you will spend time having to sort out your own thoughts when you could instead be writing. Draw up a list of Peter's work in regard to:

the army and navy
finance
government and administration
the church
the nobility
the peasantry.

Under each of these headings write down whether Peter's reforms endured in the form he intended, and how much they owed to the work of Peter's predecessors or to previous trends in Muscovite history. Let us take the example of the nobility:

Peter attempted to westernise the nobility and to employ them in state service according to the Table of Ranks. He successfully Europeanised them and took them away from their country estates. The estrangement of noble and peasant was to be a feature of Russian society until the twentieth century. In this respect, therefore, his work of reform was not superficial but of lasting and decisive importance. However, his reign only accelerated tendencies. During the seventeenth century, a westernised court nobility was beginning to emerge anyway, as represented in the person and palace of Prince Golitsyn. The peasantry were already enserfed and tied to the land and their status was already far inferior to that of their masters. The dvoriane had traditionally sought employment in the service of the ruler. What Peter did therefore was not original. By the Table of Ranks he simply speeded up and strengthened developments which were already evident.

Using this example as a model, apply the same technique of investigation to the other categories. Once you have completed this task, give your own verdict on Peter's overall achievement.

Source-based questions on 'Peter the Great, Poland and the Ukraine'

1 Mazeppa and Charles XII

Read the explanation given by Mazeppa for his defection to the King of Sweden on pages 106 and look at the map on page 107 illustrating the route of Charles XII's invasion of Muscovy. Answer the following questions:

a) What reasons does Mazeppa give in the extract for his decision to join forces with Charles XII? Explain with reference to the map what other circumstances may have compelled Mazeppa to give help to Charles.

b) Why did Charles XII decide to break off his advance in

September 1708 and to retire southwards into the Ukraine?
c) What were the consequences of Mazeppa's defeat for the Cos-
    sacks of the east-bank Ukraine and of the Zaporozhian Host?

2 The Work of Peter the Great
Read the text of Peter's speech given on page 112 and the
Archbishop of Novgorod's funeral oration on pages 112 to 113.
Answer the following questions:
a) What evidence do you know to support Peter's claim in the first
    extract that 'those whom we did not know in the light now
    respect us' (lines 2–3)?
b) Explain the references in the Archbishop's sermon to:
    i) 'the building and launching of ships' (line 4)
    ii) 'new intellectual disciplines' (lines 9–10)
    iii) 'ranks and titles' (line 13)
    iv) 'the improvements introduced into our external appearance'
        (lines 15–16).
c) How reliable do you judge the Archbishop's speech to be as
    evidence of the attitudes of Russians generally towards the work
    of Peter the Great?

Further Reading

The following general histories of Russia are all highly readable and are recommended without hesitation:

Lionel Kochan and Richard Abraham, *The Making of Modern Russia* (Penguin Books, Second Edition, 1982)
Richard Pipes, *Russia Under the Old Regime* (Penguin Books, 1977)
Nicholas V. Riasanovsky, *A History of Russia* (Oxford University Press, Fourth Edition, 1984)

Rather more detailed studies of the period 1462–1724 are available in:

Robert O. Crummey, *The Formation of Muscovy 1304–1613* (Longman, 1987)
Paul Dukes, *The Making of Russian Absolutism 1613–1801* (Longman, 1982)
Paul Hellie, *Enserfment and Military Change in Muscovy* (University of Chicago Press, 1971)

For Peter the Great:

M. S. Anderson, *Peter the Great* (Historical Association pamphlet, 1969). This provides a brief but valuable introduction.

Additional material on Peter's reign may be found in:

M. S. Anderson, *Peter the Great* (Thames and Hudson, 1978)
Robert K. Massie, *Peter the Great. His Life and World* (Victor Gollancz, 1981)

For Poland:

Adam Zamoyski, *The Polish Way* (John Murray, 1987). This provides a comprehensive narrative survey. Rather more unconventional and exciting is:

Norman Davies, *God's Playground. A History of Poland, Volume I* (Oxford University Press, 1981)

For the Ukraine the standard narrative histories are:

M. S. Hrushevsky, *A History of the Ukraine* (Yale University Press, 1941)

W. E. D. Allen, *The Ukraine. A History* (Cambridge University Press, 1940)

For the history of the Cossacks:

Philip Longworth, *The Cossacks* (Constable, 1969)

For a brief survey of Polish, Livonian and Ukrainian history:

Orest Subtelny, *Domination of Eastern Europe. Native Nobilities and Foreign Absolutism, 1500–1715* (McGill-Queen's University Press, 1986)

Sources on Russia, Poland and the Ukraine 1462–1725

A number of compendiums of source material relating to Muscovy and early Russian history have been published. Of these, the most readily available are:

L. E. Berry and R. O. Crummey (eds), *Rude and Barbarous Kingdom, Russia in the Accounts of Sixteenth-Century European Voyagers* (University of Wisconsin Press, 1968)
A. Cross (ed.), *Russia Under Western Eyes 1517–1825* (Elek Books, 1971)
B. Dmytryshyn (ed.), *Medieval Russia. A Sourcebook, 900–1700* (Dryden Press, Second Edition, 1973)
J. L. Fennell (ed.), *Correspondence Between Prince A. M. Kurbsky and Tsar Ivan IV of Russia 1564–1579* (Cambridge University Press, 1955)
J. L. Fennell (ed.), *Prince A. M. Kurbsky's History of Ivan IV* (Cambridge University Press, 1965)

Both books edited by J. L. Fennell should be treated with caution and read in conjunction with:

Edward L. Keenan, *The Kurbskii–Groznyi Aprocrypha* (Harvard University Press, 1971)

References to the works of the Marquis De Custine are taken from:

P. P. Kohler (ed.), *Journey of Our Time* (George Prior Publishers, 1980)

Documentary material in English translation relating to the history of Poland and the Ukraine is scanty. However, still for public loan in a number of places is:

Bernard Connor, *The History of Poland in Several Letters*, 2 vols (London, 1698)

It may be obtained through the inter-library loan service administered by borough libraries.

Glossary

These are the terms most commonly used in the text

dvoriane   collective name for the 'service-nobility' of Muscovy: the hereditary class of warriors and office-holders deriving from the *pomeshchiki* (see page 70).

Hetman   elected Cossack commander.

latifundia   large estates worked by serf labour.

liberum veto   right of any single deputy attending the Polish *Seym* to defeat a proposal put before the Chamber of Deputies (see page 55).

Metropolitan   head of the Russian orthodox church from the tenth to the fifteenth century. Appointed and consecrated by the Patriarch of Constantinople. Originally based in Kiev, the Metropolitan moved to Moscow in 1326. Replaced by the Patriarch of the Russian Orthodox Church in 1589.

opprichnina   literally 'a widow's portion'; that part of Muscovy which Ivan IV placed under his direct authority between 1565 and 1572 and which was administered by the **opprichniki** or 'children of darkness'.

Patriarch   head of the Russian Orthodox Church from 1589 to 1700, when Peter the Great chose to leave the office unfilled. Reconstituted by the Provisional Government in 1917.

pomeste   land held from the ruler of Muscovy in return for service, usually of a military kind. Owners of *pomeste*-land were called **pomeshchiki**.

prikazy   chanceries, or offices of state, used in the central administration in Muscovy.

Seym   the Polish parliament or diet. Met in two houses:
                            the Senate and the Chamber of Deputies. Repre-
                            sentatives sent to the Chamber were chosen at
                            local gatherings of nobility known as **seymiki**.
                            (See pages 52 to 54.)

starshina   Cossack council which advised the Hetman and
                            which comprised the wealthier Cossacks.

szlachta   collective term given to the nobility of Poland
                            and of the Polish–Lithuanian Commonwealth.

voevodas   military governors appointed by the Tsar to
                            oversee police and judicial functions in the pro-
                            vinces.

votchina   allodial or freehold property in Muscovy, owned
                            outright rather than conditionally.

Zemski Sobor   'National Assembly' which developed in the first
                            half of the seventeenth century. (See page 70.)

Acknowledgements

The publishers would like to thank the following for their permission to reproduce copyright material:

Constable for **Philip Longworth:** *The Cossacks*; Dryden Press for **Basil Dmytryshyn:** *Medieval Russia. A Sourcebook, 900–1700*; Victor Gollancz for **Robert K. Massie:** *Peter the Great. His Life and World*; Holt, Rinehart and Winston, Inc. for Excerpts from *Medieval Russia, A Source Book, 900–1700*, Second Edition, copyright © 1973 Holt, Rinehart and Winston, Inc.; Macmillan Publishers Limited for **James Cracraft:** *The Church Reform of Peter the Great*; John Murray (Publishers) for **Jan Zamoyski:** *The Polish Way*; A. B. Nordiska Bokhandeln for **Claes Peterson:** *Peter the Great's Administrative and Judicial Reforms: Swedish Antecedents and the Process of Reception*; Oxford University Press for **Norman Davies:** *God's Playground. A History of Poland, Volume I*; Penguin for **Lionel Kochan:** *Making of Modern Russia;* Thames and Hudson for **M. S. Anderson,** *Peter the Great.*

The publishers would like to thank the following for their permission to reproduce copyright illustrations:

Novosti Press Agency, page 74; The British Library, page 27; The Kobal Collection, page 46; PMT, pages 56 and 94; The Mansell Collection, page 98.

Index